A BRAVE HEART

An inspiring story of
courage, hope, and recovery

ISBN 978-1-7352818-0-3

Cover design and typesetting by Mario Lampic

Cover photo:
"The Chutes, Mt. Rose Ski Resort" by Scott Sady

A BRAVE HEART

An inspiring story of
courage, hope, and recovery

By

WILLIAM WALLACE
with
LORI HETHERINGTON

To my wife, Jill, who did the impossible.
By keeping our marriage together, she also kept our family together.
With love and gratitude.

"When health is absent, wisdom cannot reveal itself, art cannot manifest, strength cannot fight, wealth becomes useless, and intelligence cannot be applied."

Herophilus

TABLE OF CONTENTS

INTRODUCTION

by Dr. Warren D. King, MD

This book details a journey of recovery following a major trauma, a long journey with an unknown outcome. It started as a fight for survival, requiring courage and an ability to endure severe pain, and later involved commitment to far-reaching goals. The story of a man who feared losing his wife, family, friends and business. A man who eventually found assets in his impairments and new, heightened sensations in his altered body.

During the afternoon of New Year's Eve 2008 I was getting ready for an evening of celebration with my wife and friends when my phone rang. My first reaction was to feel annoyed—I'd left work early and had hoped to enjoy a relaxing holiday. When I saw the name of my best friend's wife on the display I smiled, figuring they were probably calling to exchange New Year's wishes.

"Hi, what's up, Jill? Happy New Year."

"Bill's had an accident." I could hear tension and tears.

After decades of habit, I automatically switched into emergency doctor mode, blanking out the world around me and fully concentrating on her voice. "What happened?"

She outlined the basic details and I involuntarily gasped. "Is he okay?"

"He's alive and sedated. He's having surgery tomorrow."

I sat down and took a breath. Bill Wallace has been my best friend since we were in the second grade, forty-six years ago. He's like a brother to me and I was acutely aware that my brother was in big trouble. "We'll be there as soon as we can." I hung up the phone and, for a moment, allowed myself to cry. I couldn't imagine Bill in a wheelchair.

As an orthopedic surgeon, I have worked with and cared for many patients with spinal cord injuries and have seen firsthand the devastation that can occur in the moments following major injuries and disease. We are all susceptible.

I immediately flashed back to when we were both nine years old, together learning to ski. Later we learned to face steep slopes and moguls. As adults, we'd helicopter skied in the Canadian Rockies. Bill had always been a great skier, and always pushed himself to his limits.

Introduction

My wife and I went straight to the intensive care unit as soon as we arrived at the hospital. I first gave Jill a big hug, then approached the bed where Bill was lying. He was sedated, the usual support machines blinking and humming nearby. I set my hand lightly on his shoulder. "Bill, it's Warren. We're going to get you through this. I love you, brother."

On our way to the hospital I'd spoken with a medical school classmate who gave me some tips that could help me evaluate Bill's MRI and CT scans. When the radiologist on call at the hospital pulled up the images on the computer, I recognized what I saw. The scans were similar to those of patients I'd cared for who were paralyzed.

Back in the ICU, I confirmed to Jill that I agreed, surgery was needed and it had to be performed as soon as possible. I did not tell her what I feared.

In my orthopedic practice of over thirty years, I've had the opportunity to observe patients as they deal with the challenges of injuries and aging. Many go through immense, overwhelming, and unimaginable suffering and loss of their physical health. Oftentimes they feel very depressed about their losses and obsess about what they had and what they looked like in the mirror "before".

If we live long enough, we all eventually lose most of our physical abilities. First we lose the ability to run and jump. Walking, seeing, hearing, sleeping well, and making love slip away too, perhaps sooner if we sustain serious injury. Observing my patients as they face these losses has given me perspective.

Some individuals deny their reality. They refuse to accommodate for and adjust to their changing limitations. They live in a state of "glass half empty" and are not very happy. Others do their best to maximize their abilities, seek out assistance and accept the losses they cannot overcome. Happiness comes from emerging from the devastation and finding new sources of joy.

I always urge my patients to try and turn the negatives into positives. Learn new activities and skills. Find new relationships. Educate yourself. Open yourself to the new you every day. The world has so much to offer that we can't experience it all, even if we had ten lifetimes. This is the advice I give my patients; Bill is the living proof.

A Brave Heart illustrates with powerful candor how it is possible to find meaning after trauma and inspires us to find a path out of darkness.

PROLOGUE

February 2018

I glide away from the chairlift at the top of the mountain and soak up the view, the splendor of the fresh snow. It's one of those magical mornings when every individual ice crystal glistens in the sunlight and the crisp air fills you with vitality each time you inhale.

I double check my boots and bindings, zip up my jacket, adjust my goggles and helmet, then eye my route down the slope.

Confident, I push off. My skis sink into the fresh powder and I press my shins forward against the tongue of my boots. I concentrate on coordinating my legs and upper body; the wind is in my face; my skis swoosh as they slice into snow. With each turn, the rhythm that used to be second nature slowly creeps back, seductive and frightening.

I'm feeling more and more at ease in the world I'd loved so much, but I'm not here to prove nothing's changed or act the tough guy who can't be broken. I'm on this slope to come to terms with the force that ended one part of my life almost ten years ago and face it from where I stand in my new reality. I'm getting back on the proverbial horse.

It's close to midday now and an exhilarated grin stretches across my face as my sons and I start the hike toward the parking lot.

"I knew this day would come, Dad. I knew it."

I turn to look at Craig. His eyes are overflowing with tears. And so are mine.

ONE

FIRST STEPS

December 30, 2008

"Go for help, Craig! I'm really, really hurt… I can't feel my legs." Craig's face is close to mine. I can feel his breath on my cheek, I can see the shock in his eyes.

When the paramedics finally arrive they check for a neck injury but don't find any evidence. There's no doubt about the spinal cord injury. They slide a spine board under me, hook me up to the snowmobile and drag me down the mountain. As we approach the lodge I can hear the helicopter coming in. Craig is with me as they take me off the sled and shift my body, still attached to the board, into the helicopter. They hoist me up and I connect with my son. "I think I can feel a little something," I say meekly. I have to give him some sense of hope, I've got to reassure Craig that things are going to be okay.

The medics pull the helicopter door shut and the blades begin to whir.

Oh my God. I'm gonna be in a wheelchair. Is my wife going to want to still be my wife? I'll know where we stand when I see Jill's face. I *need* to see her face.

As they roll me into the emergency room at the hospital in Reno, our eyes meet. Her lips don't move. I read "I'm in no matter what," in her gaze. But I wonder, how bad am I? What's it going to mean for her, for our kids, for our future?

The medical staff whisk me into the high level trauma center where my clothes are cut off and they drape a gown over my naked body.

A doctor approaches and pulls what appears to be a sharp poker from his pocket. He lifts the gown over my lower body and genitals. From the movement of his arm it would seem he's probing. "Can you feel that?"

"Feel what?"

He shifts position. He must be poking into my ass but I can't feel anything. "What about this?" I shake my head and want to cry.

One of my greatest fears has always been to end up in a wheelchair. Even before the accident, I'd confessed to my family and closest friends that if I ever ended up in one

I would kill myself. My very being was bonded with my mobility and I couldn't fathom separating the two.

I was terrified. My back was broken and my internal organs battered. I was in so much pain that whenever the medical staff had to move my body to perform an exam or other procedure, my wife couldn't stand to hear my screams and ran from the room. The fear of losing the freedom to walk was so fierce I could barely breathe.

Neurosurgeon Dr. Jay Morgan had plans to watch the Rose Bowl on television on New Year's Day 2009. An Ohio State alumnus, he instead spent almost twelve hours in the operating room bent over my damaged body.

The CT scan of my lower back revealed the main problem. Bone fragments were putting pressure on my spinal cord and nerves.

The surgical plan was to enter through my left side, between my lower rib and hip, cutting through tissue and muscle to expose my spinal column so that he could remove the fragments. He would then place steel rods and screws above and below the injured area and position a titanium cage to fuse the spine. There was a chance that he might have to close me up, roll me over and make another incision in my back to complete the proper anchoring. That would mean two major surgeries consecutively.

I knew the post surgical trauma involved would be massive, no matter what.

I remember them rolling me into surgery. I'd never witnessed an operating room like it. There were at least a dozen people crowding around, specialists intent on preparing for what was about to take place. The level of intensity on everyone's face made me think of jurors just before they hand the verdict to the judge in a murder case. Shifting me from the gurney onto the operating table provoked the horrific pain that I now associated with even the slightest movement. A thousand knives stabbing up my butt as searing agony travelled down my legs.

By that point in my life I'd already faced about fifteen surgeries over a period of more than thirty years, mostly due to sports injuries. I knew the routine. But this was different. I'd careened down a double black-diamond ski run that was almost four football fields long and the threat of shopping for a wheelchair was descending over me like a thick fog.

I woke up from surgery nearly half a day later. I felt as if I were drowning. My lungs couldn't take in the air I needed, as if something were blocking the in-flow; I couldn't move my body. *Help! Please, somebody help me!* I wanted to scream.

But then, I realized Jill and my three sons were there by my side. They assured me Dr. Morgan had gotten the results he'd wanted, without having to make the second incision. Tears of intense joy began to flow and, as a family, we rejoiced for this bit of good news.

Tentatively, I moved my torso slightly from side to side and discovered that the blinding, stabbing pain I had before the operation was gone. Like a miracle, Dr. Morgan's intervention had stabilized my spine. I felt like a gladiator stepping back into the arena—I had a chance to reclaim my life.

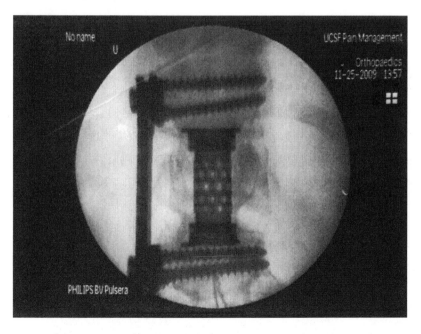

X-ray image of the hardware implanted in my back
on January 1, 2009.

When a traumatic event happens in a person's life, firsts set the tempo to the passage of time: the first time sitting up, the first solid food, the first time sleeping through the night. Each achievement means starting over in a new reality, relearning things that had previously been automatic and seeing the world from a different perspective.

Two days before my surgery, I'd pushed off from the top of a ski slope at the Mount Rose Ski Resort nestled among the Sierra Nevada mountains, the physical divide between California and Nevada. Unknowingly, that was a first step. At the time I thought I was about to ski down an exhilarating run, to bask in a shared experience with my son who was out visiting from back East and was on his own skis behind me, to barrel down the slope as the winter sun glistened on the snow, warming and eventually melting the mounds of fluffy white caught on the branches of the trees.

Within the space of a few turns of my skis, I discovered that instead, *this* first step was propelling me toward something completely unexpected.

The medical report gave the facts: *The patient was evaluated by the trauma team and was treated for multiple rib fractures, liver laceration, sacral fracture and L-1 burst fracture resulting in complete obliteration of the spinal column; neurogenic bladder, bowel, and sexual function.* In other words, I was paralyzed, unable to feel or control anything from the waist down.

While my spinal cord injury got most of the attention, there were many other parts of me that needed treatment. I couldn't urinate, my breathing was nowhere near efficient, and I couldn't control my bowels. The radiologist at the hospital told my wife he'd never seen images like mine that were not associated with permanent paralysis. However, some movement had appeared in my toes an hour or so after I was admitted to the hospital and, although it wasn't much, it offered a glimmer of hope. The expression "something is better than nothing" took on new meaning.

Jill told me afterwards that all she could think about was that I was alive and that my life was not in danger. We would deal with everything else later. She's like that—strong, proud, private, practical. Qualities that attracted me to her when we first met and that I have come to rely on in ways I never imagined.

My friends joke—with envy I'm sure—that Jill has another incredible quality that makes her stand out. "How the hell, Wallace, did you get so lucky to marry a woman who loves to watch ESPN more than you do?!" It always makes me smile.

So with this amazing woman by my side, just days short of my 52nd birthday, I began the long process of dealing with a significant spinal cord injury.

My family and I quickly learned about spinal column anatomy and physiology. Essentially the human spinal column is divided into four sections, starting from the top: there are seven vertebrae in the cervical section, twelve in the thoracic section, five in the lumbar area, and the final section is the sacral area that has five vertebrae. All together, there are thirty-three cylindrical vertebrae, each one stacked on top of the other like building blocks protecting the spinal cord which is threaded through the center.

The spinal cord transmits messages to and from the brain to control limbs, trunk, and internal organs. It's something like a super highway running through a tunnel with numerous on- and off-ramps. If one of the ramps is damaged, the traffic can't flow smoothly in that direction. If the tunnel caves in, communication comes to a screeching halt. In my case, ninety percent of the space available for the spinal cord and nerves to the legs and groin had been closed off.

Essentially, the tunnel had collapsed and my L-1 vertebra had shattered, leaving the corresponding sections of my spinal cord exposed and vulnerable. Since that's where most people's spinal cord terminates, it was a question of millimeters as to whether I would retain my mobility or not. The impact provoked by the accident had forced my spine to flex forward with such force that the bone exploded, sending fragments into my spinal cord and nerves.

The central nervous system, which is made up of the brain and the spinal cord, is so crucial to survival that it is better protected than any other organ in the body. At the same time, it's highly complex, and some of the specialized cells that make it up cannot repair themselves after an injury.

When the spinal cord is injured it goes into what's called spinal shock. For twenty-four hours the spinal cord and nerves do not function below the level of injury. The shock then resolves and it becomes possible to determine if there is complete or partial paralysis. And so, we waited to find out the extent of the lasting damage and what sort of function I would or wouldn't recover.

The first time I stood up—about a week after the accident—was when I realized how many tubes they had coming out of me: a catheter, IVs, surgically-inserted

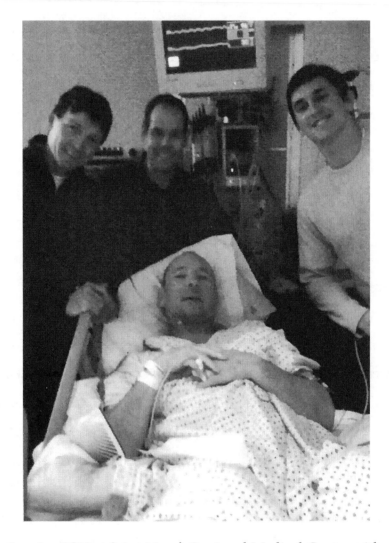

Leaving ICU at Saint Mary's Regional Medical Center with
friends Warren King and Mike Piotrowicz and son Bret by
my side, January 3, 2009.

drainage tubes for my lung and back. Each one perform-
ing a special duty to keep me in a delicate balance, but uncomfortable as hell. I hesitantly extended my legs and rose

from the bed while nurses supported me. The dizziness was overpowering. It was all I could handle for this first of firsts. They carefully eased me back onto the mattress. It wasn't much but it was a start.

Over the subsequent days, the nurses urged me to do a little bit more each time I stood up—a single step, then two. But in order to make it possible, they had to lift, unravel and arrange all the tubes so they stayed properly attached to me while hanging from my walker. It took a monumental effort each and every time.

Toward the end of week two, gripping my trusty walker and with my family urging me on, I started going out into the hallway. I'd never considered equating a hospital corridor with Grand Central Station, but that's what it seemed like. Medical staff intent on carrying out their duties going in every direction, nurses talking over their shoulder while multitasking, obstacles right and left, the voice over the PA system. The confusion as well as my own effort, fear, relief, weakness, hope, and a considerable drug load overwhelmed my senses but I had no intention of giving up. Could it be that the threat of a wheelchair was no longer staring me in the face?

There's a photo of me on one of my first forays into the hall. A hard plastic, grey "turtle shell" is strapped around my torso to protect my reconstructed spine and I'm leaning on my walker, the array of machinery, tubes and sacks hanging from the crossbar. My expression, like that of my middle son Bret in the background, is one of focused concentration. My shoulders are tense and my gaze is fixed on the linoleum floor, charting where each single step will land. I remember feeling both excited and scared as hell.

I've reflected many times over the years on one particular moment from those days in the hospital when I was learning to walk again. I'd made decent progress and was up to maybe thirty or forty steps back and forth in the corridor. One day, I passed by my surgeon, Dr. Morgan. He said, "I'm very, very happy to see you doing this." At the time I thought, *What's the big deal? I'm getting better and this is just part of what I need to do.* But later I realized he was referring to the fact that I was walking at all. I think he had expected me to have at least some paralysis and that was his way of expressing how very close I had come to losing my mobility.

With each day at the hospital, my confidence grew and my legs were able to take more of my weight. This meant I didn't have to lean on the walker as much and I was cheered by my progress. On the flip side, however, one day the medical staff discovered my right lung wasn't functioning properly. So just a day after I was freed from the tube in my left lung, they inserted another tube in the other lung. My youngest son, Joe, and brother Mike were in the room with me for the procedure; my wife and sister-in-law couldn't bear to watch. "Nasty and very cool," is how twenty-year-old Joey described it. Although I comprehended why it had to be done, torment and misery were the words I would have chosen.

There was no denying it. It was going to take a long time to recover my health.

After absorbing the initial shock, Jill started sending out daily emails to family and friends. It was a good way to keep people who cared in the loop. Her messages ranged from comments like, *I know my husband is a strong son of a bitch who's up to the challenge of yet another fight to get healthy,* to *Tears of fear have been replaced by tears of joy* when a second surgery was deemed unnecessary. Upbeat and optimistic about my progress, her messages tended to skip over the profound sense of apprehension we all felt but were afraid to express.

There are approximately 17,000 new spinal cord injuries in the United States every year and about 300,000 individuals in the US who continue to live with a spinal cord injury. Statistically, people with a spinal cord injury are anywhere from two to five times more likely to die prematurely.

We couldn't gloss over the reality of my injury. Whatever progress I'd make, whatever movement or sensation I might recover, the fact remained that this would be with us for life. Each of us had our own private way of acknowledging that complete recovery was not possible, but that didn't stop our determination to strive for the best outcome.

Jill's presence while I was hospitalized, day in and day out, was a huge help. Polite but insistent, she was a powerful advocate and made sure that I had what I needed. For example, she was quick to call for assistance when I dirtied the bed sheets, which happened daily due to my lost bowel control. Pride and privacy were gone; dignity had jumped ship. Victims of the trauma, like me.

She also helped me with my first shower. I think everyone enjoys the pleasurable sensations of a shower after they've been unable to bathe for some days. In my case, it was simply exhausting. I couldn't stand up on my own and so, after unhooking everything, I sat in a wheelchair under the shower nozzle. For us both to see my nude body in its entirety was one more shock. The bruising on my ass, between and down the back of my legs was the blackest black mixed with the reddest red. Jill wrote in an email, *I've never seen a hue of purple so deep and so dark as the color of my husband's skin.*

Jill lovingly scrubbed me down from head to toe. Well, she didn't actually scrub since she was afraid of hurting me. I was afraid too. Thank God she was there, she made me feel safe. My senses were a jumble of heightened sensitivity and dulled reactivity, like when your arm falls asleep. The slightest contact causes discomfort and, at the same time, you desperately want to move your limb but it responds sluggishly, painfully.

Finally the day came when I took my first unaided steps. "You can do it on your own now, Bill," said Brenda, the physical therapist. She pointed at my destination: a stand-alone staircase I would need to scale before I could go home. That was my finish line. It seemed miles away.

For my first unaided attempt, she had me begin in front of the staircase and walk to where my brother was standing. When I started, my forehead was bone-dry but it, along with the rest of my upper body, was drenched in sweat when I finally covered the distance. Taking those steps was the hardest thing I'd ever attempted in my life. The effort it took to get my legs to do what my brain commanded was

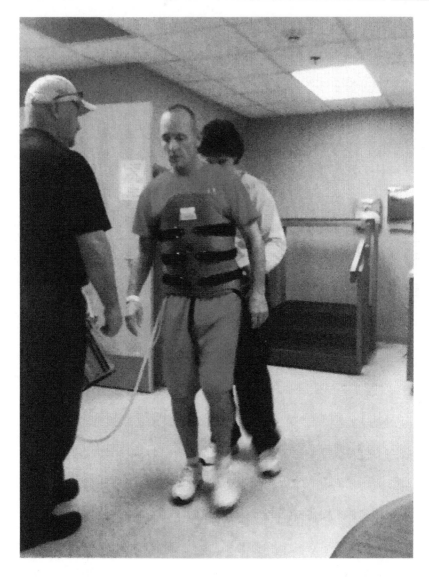

My first unaided steps on January 16, 2009.

monumental, beyond fucking hard. But I knew I had to do
it if I wanted to walk out of the hospital and head home
rather than learn how to maneuver a wheelchair. I refused

to imagine my legs as lame appendages. They were an integral part of me and I was not going to give up on them.

I took one slow, methodical step at a time in the physical therapy room. Each movement of a foot brought on a balancing act, as if I were walking on a narrow ledge. I watched my legs—the limbs I feared would never move again—as one and then the other lurched, swung, shifted forward. I was an adult-sized toddler. Each muscle movement seemingly in slow-motion, each step forward a victory. My desire to walk was like sunlight through a magnifying lens, so intense it could burn.

I wanted to shout, "Hey, everybody, look at me! I've got a chance!" Our team was behind but I might just pull out a win, like I did on the football field when I was playing for the University of Nevada Reno and I intercepted a pass in the final seconds of the homecoming game. Jubilation erupted around me in the stadium, the game was over and we'd won. But in *this* game, there was still time on the clock and I was committed to making the most of it.

I wasn't the only one who let out a huge sigh of relief on that day in physical therapy. Jill wrote in her daily email, *Bill's therapy today included taking his first steps without the walker. I honestly think I was the most nervous person in the room. I wish I could bottle his determination—we could make millions!* Her presence and unyielding support were constant. When she'd walk into my hospital room in the morning, her face alight with love, I felt as if she was the glowing orb of the sun, radiating the warmth and energy that a living being needs to survive.

Our three sons, Craig, Bret and Joe, were also there when I took my first steps and I was so grateful. By then they were men, no longer boys, and I needed them to see with their own eyes that I was fighting. Golf, tennis, cycling, skiing: with my accident, our ways of being together were wiped off the board and none of us could imagine what would take their place. But I was their dad and nothing could take that away. I needed them to know I was fixed on giving my recovery every ounce of strength I had, and that I would still endeavor to be a role model for them.

It was true that my physical recovery had begun when they rolled me out of surgery—my broken bones ever so slowly beginning to heal, blood circulating in my body, carrying oxygen and nutrients to my internal organs so they could repair themselves—but it wasn't until I took those first steps on my own that recovery became a real possibility in my mind. They were tangible evidence of the most important four-letter word: HOPE. Because recovery means having hope. Hope that there will be improvement. Hope that you won't always have to stay in a hospital bed, aided by strangers. Hope that you will eventually return to doing things for yourself. Hope that the future will, somehow, be brighter.

None of us knew what sort of progress I might be able to make. I had taken my first steps, physically and figuratively, and I intended to continue forward. A first step is what puts things in motion. It's the initial movement toward a destination. A destination that may turn out to coincide with what's imagined, or that may not. We were covering unexplored terrain and I was determined to press on.

Jill had taken her first steps too; her commitment was unwavering. In mid-January she wrote, *Again I remind myself just how incredibly lucky we are to have him working every day to learn to walk and climb stairs. I remember looking down at him in his wet ski clothes in the ER, just thinking we will love him no matter what.*

After more than three weeks in the hospital, I got the okay to transfer to a rehab center. It felt like a reason to celebrate, but the hard work—physical, emotional, and psychological—was really just beginning.

There's a picture of Jill and I taken two weeks later, thirty-five days after my accident. Of course, we're both smiling—we were getting ready for me to finally go home. Jill's blue eyes reflect her exhaustion but I can see her relief too. The hospital environment can be tough, not only for the patient who's obliged to stay there but for their spouse or parents who are providing constant support. There's rarely any privacy and the messiness of mixed emotions and adrenaline means that every fiber is taut; full, deep, calming breaths are elusive. I'm wearing my turtle shell and what appears to be a natural smile. I was just so anxious to get home that I'd forced all negative thoughts into a dark corner. We reveled in having survived those first five weeks and were anxious to get back to our home in Lafayette, California. I was thinking about seeing my black Labrador, Chipper, who was waiting for me. I was ready to return to some semblance of normality away from the discomfort of the hospital, and to have control over my daily routine. In the background there's a silly skeleton wearing an Indiana Jones hat, like a prediction of the trial-by-fire adventure that lay ahead.

TWO

PREPPING FOR THE BIG GAME

He keeps pushing himself in his daily therapy
sessions and by the time this is done, he will have
redefined the word TRAINING.

(From Jill's email, January 17, 2009)

Very few people go through life unscathed. I certainly haven't and am well aware that other people have suffered far worse than I have. My hope is that my unique combination of experiences can provide support to other individuals facing a major setback.

Like most people who are faced with adversity, I struggled and had days when I thought I'd never succeed. The myriad of physical and emotional challenges felt overwhelming and the knowledge that spinal cord injuries rarely recover fully threatened my delicate balance.

Recovery rarely proceeds in a simple linear fashion; some days are better than others. For a week you might feel like you're ready to hike fifty miles and the next day you can barely get out of bed. There may be physical gains but in parallel emotionally you feel like you're at the bottom of a well. I'm convinced that ultimately it's not the sequence of events that's key but rather your approach to the pursuit of recovery, with preparation for the difficult times a critical part of the formula.

I was the first of four children in an average middle-class family in what's known as the "Biggest Little City in the World": Reno, Nevada. With the Truckee River nearby and limitless sports facilities available, it was a wonderful place to grow up for an active and adventurous boy like me. And my parents, Bill and Mardelle, provided me with a strong moral compass.

I always had a ball in my hand—a baseball in spring and summer, a football in late summer and fall, a basketball in winter. If I wasn't out playing, I was on our rotary telephone, dialing up guys who I thought might be able to meet at the park for a pick-up game.

On the playing field, heated verbal exchanges were frequent about whether a runner was safe or out, or a football was caught out of bounds, but they usually were brief as we all knew that the longer we argued, the less time we had to play the game before we had to go home. There were no parents around to oversee the disputes and we had to handle disagreements on our own. We had no idea of how much we were learning about life.

When the time came to head home for dinner, I would toss my mitt, a couple of wooden baseball bats, five or six worn out hard balls, and the two or three old t-shirts we used as bases into a bucket which I hung over the handlebars of my bike and hit the road. It didn't matter if a cold wind blew down from the mountains or dusk was approaching: I was happy, dirty, and enjoying life.

Arguably the most fun of all was when I woke up in the morning to find the ground covered with snow. If it was a school day, the moment the lunch bell rang my friends and I would wolf down our sandwiches and spend the next fifty minutes playing tackle football on the snow-covered grass. Stumbling back into class with red cheeks and eyes wild with adrenaline didn't make our afternoon classes any easier to bear, but the joy and exhilaration that came from those games was unforgettable.

I was a small, skinny kid and sports—anytime, anywhere—were my passion. However, when it came to playing on an organized team, I had a specific goal in mind: to be in the starting line-up. And because of my small stature, that meant I had to overachieve.

When I was twelve years old I was an average baseball player, mostly because I lacked the physical maturity that some of the other boys had. But what I did have was drive and I took my ambition to the next level. I needed to figure out a way to overcome the physical obstacle, to transform myself from somebody who might be in the starting line-up to one of the guys who not only would start but would dominate the game.

I became intrigued with the role of the pitcher while watching the Saturday Major League game of the week on TV. I studied how the pitchers gripped the ball and how the trajectory or speed varied with each launch. My uncle Ray showed me how to position my two fingers over the stitching on the ball and twist as I released it from my hand. That ability to throw a curveball gave me the edge I needed on the baseball diamond. My twelve-year-old opponents weren't used to having a ball come at their head that then, as they ducked out of the way, would swerve back over the plate before disappearing into the catcher's glove. "Striiiike!" I froze batter after batter at the plate. Not bad for a skinny preadolescent.

Little did I know then that the art of throwing a curveball while my joints, tendons, and ligaments were not yet fully developed would take its toll.

The distance between the mound and home plate was forty-five feet according to league rules for my age bracket. As I got older the distance increased to sixty feet, meaning that my arm came under even greater stress.

As I entered high school, the first of my many injuries occurred. Thanks to that injury—which I can say only now—I started learning about recovery.

My throwing arm was subjected to incredible torque and hyperextension and bone chips had begun drifting in and out of my elbow joint. It got to the point that I couldn't straighten my arm and had to bend and extend it rapidly until the chips drifted out of the joint. I didn't speak to my parents or coach about my problem because I was afraid they wouldn't let me play, but my guess is that they tried to talk to me about it. I was so focused on playing back then that I ignored everything else. Eventually my clever adaptation—or what I thought was clever—didn't work anymore.

Surgery was the only way to fix it. As a result, I missed my junior year of high school baseball. Having to watch my friends from the sidelines was torture. With every pitch, my muscles contracted as if I were out there throwing the ball or standing in the batter's box. I felt helpless, banished from wearing a uniform and expelled from the game. If I wanted to get back on the field for my senior year, I would have to follow every detail of the rehabilitation program the doctor gave me. I knew exactly what I wanted, and so I did everything I could to recover as quickly as possible.

To be a valuable player on a baseball team, it's not enough to be good in your defensive position. Making consistent, solid contact with the ball when you're at bat is an attention getter no matter what level of ball you're playing. And during my adolescent years, I got massive amounts of batting practice in my backyard with my brothers and friends.

The joy of physical activity has always been in my blood, it's a family trait I share with my two brothers and sister; sports were central to our growing up.

We lived in a modest house and our yard was rectangular. We set up home plate toward the back, with a chaise lounge tipped on its side as a backstop. First base was near the chimney, second was opposite home plate, marked by bare dirt where we'd killed off the grass with our sneakers, and third was the juniper bush across from the chimney.

But the most important part of the whole equation was the ball itself.

We couldn't use a normal baseball or even a tennis ball because the backyard was too small. This left us with two options: not play in the yard at all or find an alternative. We chose the latter and played with a wiffle ball—that plastic cut-out marvel that saved our house from broken windows. With practice we learned to make that wiffle ball dance and sing. In addition, the plastic wiffle ball bat, about half the size of a regular baseball bat, helped train our hand-eye coordination as we pitched to each other for hours on end. If you could hit a darting, curving wiffle ball with a spindly bat, a baseball was a cinch with a standard bat in hand.

All this practice and repetition was turning me into an expert hitter, teaching me that focusing on the process was the way to achieve the outcome I desired.

As much as I loved baseball, I loved football even more. I started playing Pop Warner football when I was around ten and by the time I was twelve or thirteen I was totally comfortable running into an opposing player at full speed. It didn't matter how big or how fast the other guy was, I was undaunted. I made up for being undersized with pure determination. My throwing and receiving skills had developed over the years in the same way I'd learned with baseball—in the backyard, at the park, in the snow—repeating the moves over and over until I could throw a tight spiral and hit a target or tackle a guy with my eyes closed.

When I was going into my junior year in high school, we got a new football coach and he familiarized himself with the players during the summer workouts. But for me, that summer was all about baseball and, when I wasn't playing, I was working a full-time summer job. I installed insulation in residential attics where the temperature hovered around 110°. It was hard work and pink fiberglass shreds from the insulation stuck to my sweaty skin, but it was a job. After work I would drive my car to the baseball field, change into my uniform in the backseat then run onto the diamond, taking my place at second base. By the end of the day I was hungry enough to eat a horse and so exhausted that I fell into bed, but all was right in my world.

Playing baseball that summer, though, cost me a spot on the varsity football team. When I showed up to get my football equipment in late August the coach handed me my pads and said, "Wallace, where were you all summer?"

"Playing baseball, coach."

"Tough luck, you're on junior varsity this year."

I was furious. I was just as good, if not better, than the guys who'd been put on the varsity team but that didn't matter. Instead, what I got was a huge chip on my shoulder. That year I played free safety and quarterback alongside five or six other juniors and we were full of boisterous over-confidence and grit. We were consumed by our desire to be victorious and in fact finished the season undefeated. It was actually one of the most enjoyable athletic experiences of my life.

The following year, finally on the varsity team, I played free safety. The coach also put me on the roster as back-up quarterback. I'd never been back-up anything on a playing field, and I didn't like it. The starting quarterback was bigger and stronger, a fact that triggered my deep-seated desire to overachieve.

At the end of our regular season we'd won the northern Nevada zone championship and qualified to play the southern Nevada zone champions for the state title. The playoff would take place in a big-time stadium in Las Vegas, under the lights and on Astroturf which accentuated everything, especially the speed of the game and the agility of the players.

Our starting quarterback went down with an injury in the first quarter. Then came those words I was waiting to hear, "Wallace, you're in!"

hroughout the season I had practiced as if I'd be called
o play both free safety and quarterback in each game,
unaware I was developing a character trait: always be ready.

Right off the bench, as my team's quarterback, I led us
down the length of the field on our first drive, conclud-
ing with a 12-yard quarterback bootleg run just inside the
corner pylon and into the end zone. It was the first touchdown of the game.

The other team's fullback and middle linebacker was
a beast with cat-like quickness. He weighed well over 200
pounds while I was maybe 150 pounds soaking wet. At
least a half a dozen times during the game he broke free
from the line of scrimmage, meaning I was the only one
between him and the goal line. Despite our size differenc-
es, I summoned all the strength and speed my body could
produce and went after his tree trunk-sized thighs. My
only option was to try and take his legs out from underneath him. I saw more stars during that game than I could
count. After four quarters, our stronger and faster opponents were the victors, but my performance as a defensive
player that day is what changed the course of my life.

Among the spectators, there were several college
scouts watching and in the following weeks I got a few
phone calls at home. The University of Nevada Reno was

the most persistent: they were interested in giving me a football scholarship. I asked one of their assistant coaches during the recruiting process why they wanted me to play for them. He replied, "We've never seen a free safety make so many tackles of the other team's running backs and quarterback behind the line of scrimmage." His answer was good enough for me and I was set to attend my hometown university playing the game I loved.

Although I would be going to school in the same town where I'd grown up, my father suggested that it might be a good idea to move out and learn to be independent. Honestly, I already had one foot out the door. My best friend since second grade, Warren King had also been recruited and agreed to move out with me. With our photos on the front page of the sports section of the Reno newspaper and letters of intent in hand, we were ready to conquer the world!

But playing football and baseball weren't the only things I did during my high school years. I was also falling in love with a special girl.

I'd noticed her on campus but we'd never spoken. I was in my senior year and on the football team, and she was a junior and a song leader, which meant that during pep rallies and sports events she was part of a dance troupe. She had the most spectacular dimples and smile I had ever seen, and her legs… oh man! I was totally taken by her when she was out there doing her dance routine but she seemed out of reach, over my head.

Jill Scattini, 1974.

As a Reno High School varsity football player, 1975.

Then one evening, entering a parentless house during a graduating seniors' party, I saw her. As a junior, she shouldn't have been there but I was glad she was. Here was my opportunity. We made eye contact and without either of us saying a word, I knew the game was on. We talked and flirted and charmed each other all night until I got up my courage.

"Do you want a ride home?" I asked, scraping together whatever poise I could wrestle from my nerves.

It was love at first sight, but I had some business to take care of. On the drive home I told her, "I have another girlfriend. You'll need to give me some time to break off the relationship." I couldn't be dishonest with her, I sensed there was too much at stake.

Three weeks later, we were a couple, head-over-heels in love.

Whenever I went to her house to take her out, I'd knock on the door and her mother would answer. Her father was always at work, a fact that I didn't find particularly odd in light of his job, and besides my own father had variable hours too.

The months passed, our relationship grew, and eventually the time came for commitment on the letter of intent to play football at the University of Nevada Reno. Up until then, my contacts from the university had been the assistant coaches, but the day came when the head coach came to visit me and my parents at home.

When Coach Scattini arrived, there really wasn't much to talk about since I was convinced and ready to sign. However my dad did have one question. "Why are you interested in a guy like Bill who doesn't have the physical stature to be playing Division I football?"

"Mr. Wallace," the coach replied, "your son's a winner. He knows how to win and is willing to make the necessary sacrifices. At the Division I level we're much more interested in those qualities than in the height and weight of a player."

I didn't care why they wanted me, I just wanted to play ball. And hearing the coach talk about me in that way boosted my confidence.

We sat down at the dining room table and signed all the papers. Before Coach Scattini left, I said, "Coach, I have one more thing to tell you. For the past year I've been dating your daughter, Jill."

His jaw dropped.

I explained that on the various occasions when I'd gone to pick her up he'd never been home. In those days, in fact, a Division I coach was constantly on the road either recruiting or coaching games.

So there it was. My girlfriend was the daughter of my new coach. I'd been mulling over how to handle it for a while and saw it as a no-win situation. In my eighteen-year-old mind, there was only one thing to do: I had to break up with her. I couldn't run the risk of being treated differently from any of the other guys on the team. Whatever my accomplishments, they had to be 100% earned, with no favorable treatment granted.

Too young to see any other options, I broke Jill's heart and walked away.

I stepped on the university field in August 1975 to begin the grueling schedule of two practices a day, six days a week in 100-plus degree temperatures. The physical demands tested my body and the mental rigors challenged my determination in new ways. It took every ounce of my being to survive the pre-season training period. It was the beginning of my journey from boyhood to manhood. At the time I had no idea that I would draw on that experience to carry me through the extreme adversities I would face later.

When a team has a big game coming up, they kick their training into high gear. They go through drills and practice strategic plays over and over until they've got them down pat. Looking back over my pre-accident life I can see that I, unknowingly, was training for *my* big game. Right from the beginning, during the initial weeks at the hospital, doctors and other medical professionals told me that my muscle tone and development would play an enormous role in determining what sort of recovery I might attain. Another person, same sex, same age, same accident, but with an out-of-shape body would fare far worse in terms of outcome, they asserted. Throughout the years, I've heard the same thing over and over: the level of my physical and mental conditioning prior to the trauma laid the groundwork, allowing me to recover from my spinal cord injury to the extent that I have. My years of training paid off.

It's highly likely that a setback—whether it's a life-threatening accident or illness, or an emotionally-trying event such as divorce or the loss of a loved one—is, unfortunately, going to hit just about everyone at some point. It can catch you completely unprepared, or you can keep yourself as physically and mentally fit as your body allows so that you're ready when that setback occurs. The best advice I can offer is be ready for *your* big game.

As anyone who's played team sports knows, every member on a team is important. It's the dynamic between the individuals and the encouragement they offer each other when faced with challenges that urge the team as a whole to move forward. Whenever I was on a playing field, I gave my all for the team and had no doubt that my team members would give their all for me.

That's precisely what my youngest son did.

Joe had been given a scholarship to play baseball at my alma mater. He earned it on his own merits and was proud of his accomplishment, as were Jill and I. He was in his sophomore year when I had my accident.

Attending college in Reno meant that he—like the rest of my Reno family—was on hand, frequently sitting by my bedside or cheering me on in the physical therapy room, an important part of my support team. Meanwhile, he did his best to keep up with his studies and emotionally deal with what had happened to me. But the baseball season was scheduled to start in just a few short weeks and extra practice time and games, whether at home or away, would eat into his already overloaded schedule and headspace.

He sat down with his coach and had a long talk. "I don't think I can put my heart and soul into the season, knowing what my dad's going through," my son told him. A Division I scholarship is hard to come by and giving it up was not something to take lightly.

After much thought, Joe chose to drop out and help take care of me. It was his idea. I couldn't help but feel guilty—I knew how much participation in college sports can mean to a young man—and will forever be grateful for his support. Words can't adequately describe the depth of my appreciation.

February 3, 2009 started out as a joyful day. I was being released from the rehabilitation center in Reno and we were finally going to get in the car and return to our home in the Bay Area. It seemed like a dream come true.

A straight shot from Reno to San Francisco, Interstate 80 is one of the primary east-west highways of North America and roughly traces some of the historic overland routes. The segment between Nevada and California skirts the last stretch of the California Trail, the route thousands of settlers followed in the mid-1800s, often under extreme hardship, in search of what they hoped was the promised land.

Our trek was much the same.

The two hundred miles that separate Reno from our home in Lafayette is usually a three-and-a-half-hour drive. It seemed feasible. We were hopeful that once I got home my condition would improve steadily, and that I was headed for a better life just like the early settlers.

Jill stopped her Honda CRV in front of the hospital and reclined the front passenger's seat; I stood up from the wheelchair that patients are required to use at discharge. Leaving the wheelchair behind put a smile on my face. Five weeks before, it seemed this day would never come and yet, there I was. I eased myself into the car and we set off.

It didn't take long for the smile to transform into a grimace. Every bump in the road sent pain shooting through my body. The vertebrae in the lumbar portion of my spine—the ones that suffered the worst damage—are directly linked to the nerves in the lower abdomen and legs. I screamed at poor Jill whenever she had to step on the brakes, change lanes or the tires rolled over the slightest imperfection in the pavement. One hundred percent of my focus was turned toward my own pain. Had I been able to pay attention to her I would have been aware of the torture that she, too, was enduring. A heavy dose of reality landed on us like a ton of bricks.

After five hours of hell, we pulled into our street.

The sky was cobalt blue and the hills green from the early spring grasses, but I only know that because of the picture I have of me giving a thumbs up, my smile drawn and forced. Neighbors had hung out a *Welcome home, Bill!* sign. Jill wrote in her email, *WE ARE HOME!!! Rose Lane has never looked so perfect. We are so thankful to be home; the house has never looked so good.*

Fighting the pain but needing desperately to move my legs after the grueling trip, I walked to the end of the street. Alone for a moment, I told myself, "I am *so* fucked."

When Jill and I went into the house a short while later, we climbed the stairs in silence and stepped into the bedroom we'd previously slept in as a couple. The crushing reality hit us that our lives together, as we'd known them, were over. We laid down on the bed and, for the first time since the accident, both sobbed uncontrollably.

THREE

GET COMFORTABLE
BEING UNCOMFORTABLE

Life doesn't keep track of the good things and bad things that happen to you and even them out over time. It doesn't say, "Well, you've been through a horrific health issue so now it's your turn to have some good things happen." Instead, what life handed me was one setback after another, and more than once.

About a month and a half after I got home from the hospital I experienced an excruciating bout of neuropathic pain and lower body weakness. It was worse than anything I had experienced up until then. I was terrified that my condition was deteriorating. Maybe I was experiencing acute bladder or kidney failure. Or perhaps, as the doctors had warned us occasionally occurs, the fluid that flows around the spinal cord was obstructed by the injury, causing additional damage. They'd said that it could even cause death. In tears, I called my best friend, Dr. Warren King, who owned a small private plane. "Please, get me to Reno. I'm in big trouble and I don't know what to do." If I needed more surgery or some other procedure, I didn't want anyone other than Dr. Morgan to touch me.

Two hours later in Reno my brother Mike met me at the airport and accompanied me to the emergency room.

Through clenched teeth, I begged the ER nurse to give me something for the pain. At that moment, my pain level was a 12 on a 10-point scale. She hooked up an IV and injected the drug. I watched the liquid make its way into my body and felt the pain plummet in a matter of seconds until it was completely obliterated and I was in a haze.

Meanwhile, Jill was driving as fast as she safely could from Lafayette. She bolted into the hospital at about the same time as the MRI machine was spitting out my scans.

Feeling as if the clock had been turned back, dread and apprehension gnawing at our insides, we anxiously awaited bad news. Given the incredible pain and uncontrollable convulsions of my lower body, my mind raced from one horrific prospect to another, pausing to consider the irreparable kidney damage I might suffer if my bladder stopped working, before it moved on to even more terrifying possibilities.

Dr. Morgan approached the hospital bed where I was agonizing. He explained that the trauma of my accident, and the subsequent surgery and physical therapy, had apparently combined to cause a flare up of a spinal stenosis I'd suffered, with a resulting case of drop foot, some years before. I had had a couple of steroid injections to resolve the matter and thought nothing more of it. But this time, with all that my back had recently gone through, the nerves were critically pinched. The good news was that it could be fixed surgically.

Here we go again, I thought.

On March 15, a little more than two months after my accident, I was back in the operating room for bilateral decompression of my spinal stenosis. The surgery itself was a success but I suffered from incredibly intense post-surgical back pain, layered on top of the chronic pain I was already experiencing day in and day out. I hated having to take morphine together with an opioid called Dilaudid, but I had no choice. It was a question of survival.

A few days after the surgery, I reluctantly climbed into Jill's car again and she got behind the wheel. We repeated our trip of misery.

When I was a freshman at the University of Nevada Reno, the starting free safety on our football team went down with an injury in the second half of our homecoming game against our most difficult opponent, Cal Poly San Luis Obispo. Coach Scattini called me over, "You're in, Wallace." With no warm-up, I was on the field with the task of guarding the Cal Poly tight end who was six foot eight and outweighed me by a hundred pounds. We were up by four points and they needed to score a touchdown in order to win.

The stadium was jam-packed and the fans sensed the tension.

With two minutes left on the clock and their ball on our 25-yard line, the Cal Poly quarterback dropped back to pass. Out of the corner of my eye I could see his wide receiver cutting toward the middle of the field. I planted my back foot and made a move to anticipate the pass. I leapt as high into the air as I could with my arms extended above my head and intercepted the ball. With the support of a couple of blockers in front of me, I managed to make about 25 yards along the sideline until what seemed like the entire Cal Poly offensive line came crashing on top of me. I could hear my ecstatic teammates cheering from the bench.

Once all the bodies climbed off me and I rose to my feet, I glanced toward the stands: mass hysteria. The clock had run out. Fans stormed the field as the brass and percussion sections of the band launched into a deafening version of the school fight song. Local newspaper reporters grabbed me for interviews as the melee swirled around us.

Afterwards, riding high on the emotions, I made the trek toward the locker room. Coach Scattini was waiting for me. After congratulating me he said, "There's someone who wants to see you outside after you've showered." Twenty minutes later I walked out, my hair still wet.

There was Jill, waiting for me with tears and love in her clear blue eyes. Painfully aware I'd made a mistake breaking up with her, I was overwhelmed with relief that she'd taken the lead in getting us back together. No need to convince me—this time it would be forever.

During our university years, we were apart a lot since Jill was at University of California Berkeley and I was in Reno but we remained committed. We talked on the phone every Sunday evening, because that's when it cost less, and made plans for our future together.

By the time I was a junior, there was no doubt in my mind about life after college. Jill had to be a part of it, I loved her with all my heart. She was and has always been my touchstone, the rational voice when my thoughts and eagerness get the best of me. I proposed, she accepted, and we made it official.

We set the date—July 14, 1979—and Jill and her mother started planning. I knew it was important for her to have all the pieces in place and that they would not overlook a single thing. I just wanted to be husband and wife. If anyone had asked, it would have been fine with me to get married in shorts and t-shirts surrounded by sagebrush.

I remember that by April we still hadn't found the rings. It's clear in my mind because I was playing baseball for U.N. Reno and we had an away-game against Santa Clara University. Jill had come to cheer us on. The game wasn't very exciting and, through the fence, she told me she'd be back when it finished to pick me up.

A few innings later she reappeared at the fence. "I found them! When the game's over we've got to go to the jewelry store!"

As soon as the final out was called I trotted to her car in the parking lot in my stockinged feet and filthy uniform. Cleats didn't belong in a fine jewelry store.

We bought the rings on the spot. Three months later, when we recited the traditional vows and slipped those symbols of eternal devotion onto each other's finger we could not have imagined how profoundly we would be put to the test.

With our parents on our wedding day, July 14, 1979.

I had envisioned beginning my business career in Reno where my father could mentor me, but instead we moved to Oakland, California, across the bay from San Francisco. Jill was still a student at nearby U.C. Berkeley and we decided to remain there after she graduated. The Bay Area had a thriving economy that produced well-paid employees and professionals, and successful businesses that were potential clients for me in my job as a commission-based sales representative for New York Life Insurance Company. Great opportunities awaited a young, ambitious man with a strong work ethic. But in a business where knowing people and networking are your lifeblood, being twenty-two years old and living in an area where I knew no one was a huge challenge.

My father had been a New York Life agent for more than twenty years—more or less since I was born—although for the most part I was in the dark about what he actually did on a daily basis. I knew, however, that he'd had the freedom to be a constant presence during my youth and I hoped that someday I'd be able to provide that same support for the children Jill and I dreamed of having. When my college team was playing a midweek game in some place that required several hours of driving each way to attend, my father and mother were always sitting in the stands rooting me on, often the only fans on our side of the field. Now as a married man myself, I figured if I followed his footsteps and worked hard, I'd be able to be my own boss and be present for my family too. Besides, I liked the idea of having direct control over how successful I could become.

The company provided some basic training but at the end of the day it was a question of making appointments with potential clients. I had to make as many as fifty cold calls every day when I first started in order to get the minimum two appointments a day that the experts said offered a *chance* at success. The second, and no less formidable challenge, came when I met the potential clients in person and needed to convince them to trust me in the first few minutes. Rejection was a constant menace. I never got used to it.

There aren't many people who can get kicked in the face day after day and still get back on their feet and make another cold call. Perseverance and my Dad's example were what kept me going. If he could make a good living at this job, and if I had survived preseason football training at college, then I knew I would get through this too.

I can't describe how incredibly difficult it was. For the first fifteen years, I woke up every morning with a knot in my stomach and a lump in my throat. Was I going to be able to make two appointments that day? Was I going to make enough money that month to cover our house payment? Was I going to make enough money to cover my business costs? I was scared to death most of the time and, essentially for almost twenty years, never went home on a Friday afternoon without having made, at least, ten appointments for the following week.

There's a common denominator when it comes to personal success. Successful people do the things that other people don't like to do. They knuckle down and forge forward, knowing that by doing the unpleasant, the inconvenient, the difficult, the painful, the disagreeable, there will be a reward. It's what athletes do every time they participate in a sport. Clashing with an opponent or simply one's self, fighting to overcome the hurdle in order to obtain the reward of a first down, a goal, a faster time, or the championship trophy. It really is true that sport is a metaphor for life.

One of the unpleasant things I've had to learn to accept in my recovery was having people see me in my new condition. I had to conquer my embarrassment. It was very uncomfortable for me when I hobbled into the gym for the first time after my accident with no muscle mass while leaning on a walker. After more than forty years of physical training and participation in competitive sports, I faced a feeling that I personally detested: weakness.

Not that I was unsympathetic in the face of someone in difficulty or who was struggling, but weakness was not something that sat well on me. I'd always taken pride in seeing the proof of my fitness in the mirror; suddenly the reflection felt like humiliation.

I have, however, learned to cope with weakness, although that doesn't mean I like it. Vulnerability and a lack of control over my destiny were sensations I sought to avoid at all cost. But in 2000, nearly nine years before my skiing accident, I had no choice. I came down with an infection that nearly killed me.

Anyone who has undergone surgery has had to sign the form that explains the risks of anesthesia and the one in a zillion chance you could acquire an infection or suffer some other unintended consequence. Well, I became one of those statistics.

I'd had simple back surgery and walked out of the hospital a couple of days after the operation in good spirits. I was glad to have resolved the pain and numbness in my legs that had come from a breakdown of the discs in my lower back. Around the same time, I was struggling with debilitating tendinitis in my elbows that had developed from years of overuse. The timing was right for the surgery—I figured I'd take a break from all activities for a few months and let my body rest and recover.

About three weeks later, out of the blue, I began having the most unbelievable pain in my back. I called the surgeon and asked if it was possible I'd ruptured a disc. He essentially blew me off, saying it was just post-operative pain and that in a day or two it would go away.

By that time, I'd already undergone numerous other surgeries over the years to repair ligaments in both knees, the rotator cuff in my shoulder, and the bone chips in my elbow. I'd had some experience with post-op pain. Deep down I knew something was wrong.

With Jill's help, I practically crawled to the imaging center and demanded they do a new MRI without a prescription from the doctor. Thank God they had enough compassion to agree. I also asked them to forward their report to three different doctors.

At 6:30 a.m. the following day our home phone started ringing, one call after another. The doctors' offices were phoning with the results: I had a massive staphylococcus infection and needed to get to an infectious disease center immediately. My life was at risk.

What followed can only be described as horrific.

The infectious disease specialist's first task was to match the exact bacteria causing the infection with the proper antibiotic and, in order to do so, they needed to extract a biological sample from my back.

They positioned me face down on a gurney and another doctor, who I'd never met and who didn't even greet me when he walked in the room, plunged a needle into the depths of my spine with no anesthesia. It felt as if someone had shoved me into a live electrical socket. The first attempt to collect a sample was unsuccessful. He tried a second time and again a jolt of electricity shot through my back, causing my body to lurch off the table. When even a third attempt came up empty the doctor threw the needle down and stormed out of the room. Apparently my prior surgery and infection had blocked the necessary passageway. The gurney was wheeled out of the room, with me writhing from the ordeal.

They administered Benadryl for the pain but within minutes I had a reaction. I was evidently allergic to it. I felt closer to death and in more despair than I'd ever imagined possible.

Luckily, the infectious disease doctor was a compassionate man. He reassured me, "Mr. Wallace, since we can't identify the exact bacteria we'll have to treat it as if it's the worst known type. We'll call in the big guns."

The drug, Vancomycin—or Vanco for short—had to be administered through a fixed pick line inserted into my arm that ran straight through an artery to a chamber in my heart. Every day for six weeks I had to attach a bag of Vanco to a pump, hook it up to the pick line in my arm and lie on my bed while the poison killed off the infection and, at the same time, destroyed my lower back. The pain was so excruciating I thought I would never heal.

I had never faced a setback like it. Every time I'd had an injury or an operation, I recovered by following the advice of doctors, physical therapists, and with my own perseverance. It was a given: do what you need to do and the results would follow. But this time I was terrified that I'd never recover. This was an opponent I'd never faced and I was scared to death. I only knew that the infection was virulent, potentially fatal, and that I was a wreck. Since it was systemic, it affected my entire body, as well as eating away at the soft tissues and bones at the infection site.

When the infection was finally defeated my lower back was decimated: the bone pain was debilitating and my muscles were wasted. The feeling of frailty seemed like a failure. As if I hadn't been strong enough to be victorious. As if I'd lost the game. I remember standing unsteadily in my backyard, looking up at the hill behind our house. Pre-infection I routinely jogged up it then hit the ground for a set of pushups before running back down. There was no way I would ever get up that hill again. The infection had kicked my butt like nothing else ever had. I thought I would never be strong again.

Fortunately, I was wrong.

Virtually any rehabilitation program—whether it's for a physical injury or a psychological wound—involves discomfort. It's just a fact. And I can confidently say that the sooner a person facing rehab makes peace with being uncomfortable, the sooner they can start making progress.

It took about four years of stubborn dedication and lots of hard work but I rebuilt my muscle tone and strength until I was in better physical shape than ever—I'd succeeded in rebounding from a setback that I believed was impossible to recover from. Every time I think of that experience, I'm reminded of how important it is to never give up.

When I first went to the gym after the skiing accident with my walker and atrophied body, I had to check my ego and pride at the door. If I wanted to recover my health—and I did, with all my heart—I'd have to start from square one. I took the pin out of each weight machine and put it at the easiest setting, then I did as many repetitions as I could until exhaustion. According to most trainers and physical therapists, the "one set to exhaustion" approach is an optimal strategy for strength training. It involves doing a single set of twelve to fifteen repetitions then incrementing the weight slowly over time to build muscle mass. In the beginning, I was able to do only a few repetitions before I hit exhaustion. Each exercise was painful, demanding, frustrating, and draining but I kept at it until eventually I was able to properly do a full set. Once I was able to do one full set to exhaustion, I continued doing so every single time I went to the gym. I still do. Much like making two appointments every day for twenty years.

As I was growing up, I had a coach who had two favorite sayings: "If it's worth doing, it's worth doing right" and "Focus on the execution, not the outcome." By giving your attention to the way your muscles move and the signals they send you, to the correct positioning of your body, you're concentrating on the process. This in turn allows you to do whatever is *your* best, without wasting your energy thinking about some destination you've got in your head or comparing yourself to somebody else. The coach's words have stuck with me and go hand in hand with pushing beyond my comfort zone as a way to achieve the success I desire.

It sounds pretty simple on paper, but very few people actually do it. When things get uncomfortable, most people get scared. And it's okay to be scared, but if you get paralyzed by your fear there's no way to make progress. If, however, you put yourself in a situation that really challenges your limits and do what you need to do to the best of your ability, the discomfort will slowly fade and measurable progress will take its place.

With our sons Craig, Joe, and Bret, 1996.

If someone were to ask me, "What have been the five greatest moments of your life so far?" I'd have no trouble listing the first three: being present for Craig (1984), Bret (1986), and Joe's (1989) births. The unconditional love I felt from the first moment for each of our sons is raw, fierce and absolute.

Our family has been fortunate in so many ways. Jill and I have, with great joy, watched the boys grow up in the way we'd dreamed they would. I coached every one of their youth basketball and baseball teams and Jill ran the snack shack or assumed other duties that made the teams run properly. We were committed to sharing the many virtues and life lessons that can be learned from athletic competition with our sons, like hard work, being part of a team, and having respect for the rules, your body and other individuals.

And, luckily for me, Jill—the daughter of a football coach—also understood my own need for physical challenges and the vital role sports played in my identity.

We had a small blue pickup truck during those years when the boys were young. One of my fondest memories is tossing all the baseball equipment into the back of the truck and having them jump in with the bats and balls before heading off to a practice or game. (Mind you, this was before it was illegal to transport passengers in the back of a pickup!) Our family life was active and happy.

The rigors of getting the boys in and out of their car seats when they were little, holding them between my legs to teach them how to ski and lifting them over and over up onto the chairlift began to take their toll on my back. This was also when I developed the chronic tendinitis in my right elbow. The aches and pains didn't stop me, and I continued to help not only my own sons but also all the other kids on the teams by throwing batting practice and hitting ground balls and pop-flies. Persistent inflammation eventually set in.

Like when I had the bone chips as a fifteen year old, I didn't listen to my body. When you're coaching your kids, no one else can really do it like you can; when you're playing golf with potential clients who will help you put food on the table, you push through the warning signs. I seriously regret playing deaf to the messages my body was sending me. I now understand that if you pay attention to your body it will guide you, but only if you listen to it.

However with each surgery and then the staph infection, I was unknowingly learning the art of recovery, learning to work with my body by discovering its strengths and limitations as well as my own mental cues, and how to coax it back to health.

Around the time I turned fifty, all the hard work was beginning to bear fruit. I was pain free and back out on the golf course, back on the ski runs, back playing doubles tennis. In addition, my business was prospering and finally the day-to-day pressure had eased. I'd put Craig and Bret through college and Joey had just received his baseball scholarship; I was very much looking forward to watching him develop as a college athlete.

On top of all that, Jill and I were experiencing a rebirth in our marriage. In Hawaii to celebrate our anniversary, we basked in our once-a-year opportunity to escape the rigors of the daily routine. Surrounded by the fragrance of flowers, the chorus of exotic birds, the caress of the trade winds and the warm, clear water full of tropical fish the stress faded away. After more than thirty years together, we were just as in love and connected as ever. I felt like the luckiest man in the world.

I was riding high and looking forward to what I hoped would be the most rewarding period of my life. What could possibly get in the way?

In late December 2008, Craig was home for the holidays. He'd already graduated from college and was working back East. He and I shared our strongest bond through skiing and every year around the holidays we'd go to the mountains for two or three days.

That year he'd brought a couple of college buddies home with him. There wasn't much snow yet that season, but Craig wanted to share the experience of skiing with his friends. Besides, any time he and I could hit the slopes together was special.

The guys and I got up early on the 30th while Jill still slept. We piled into the car in the dark, and drove to the Mount Rose resort in Nevada, a short distance over the state line.

When we got there, I asked at the ticket counter about snow conditions and which runs would be best. The guy said, "For you experts, the Chutes are mostly open, even if there are a few closures due to lack of snow."

We spent the morning getting Craig's friends going and giving them pointers, but I also managed to squeeze in a couple of runs down the Chutes to check out the conditions.

The Chutes section of the resort offers some of the longest, steep, north-facing slopes in North America. After many years of learning from me, Craig had grown as a skier and was now capable of handling the really challenging terrain, having already proved himself on the renowned KT-22 section at Squaw Valley, site of the 1960 Winter Olympics.

In the early afternoon my son and I were ready to hit the tough slopes and I texted Jill, "We're on our way to the Chutes." We were psyched and anxious to share the exhilaration. We were also undeterred by the sign, *Experts*

Only, at the gate to the Nightmare run at the top of the mountain.

The gate leading to the Nightmare ski run
at the Mount Rose Ski Resort. (*Photo by Scott Sady*)

I started down the hill first, a bit ahead of Craig. The first part of the run was kind of barren and low on snow but once we picked our way through that section the rest promised the excitement we'd come for. The steepness of the run is such that when you get going, you pick up speed quickly, like a skier expects on an expert slope.

I made one turn from my right to my left, and then another left to right, starting a smooth rhythm. In the middle of my third turn my ski hit something hard under the snow. The impact knocked it right off my boot.

Now with only one ski, I did my best to stay upright, shooting over the snow as I struggled to keep in control. But, instead, I gained speed. I quickly realized I was in serious trouble. I tried to dig down into the snow with my ski-less boot but to no avail.

Years of playing football had taught me how to fall and I tried to put that knowledge to good use but I just kept going faster and faster. As I was cascading down the mountain, front to back, over and over, I could see something dark approaching. Again I tried, desperately, to dig in with my boot, to change my trajectory, but I was going too fast and the slope was too steep.

I already figured I was hurt. Maybe some broken ribs but nothing too significant up to that point. However when my body slammed into the tree, my back exploded.

My momentum broken, I rolled off the trunk and slid slowly over the snow, finally coming to a stop.

When I lifted my head and torso out of the slush, my brain asked my feet and legs to move. They remained immobile. My brain ordered them to move, but still no response.

Craig had witnessed every second of the tragedy. I started to cry.

I remember the first time I hobbled into Dr. Irv Johnson's office after the accident. At that point I was using elbow crutches. "Oh my God, you're not in a wheelchair. I can't believe you're walking." He'd read the report of my injuries before I came in. If my internist of twenty years was shocked, then maybe my mobility really did border on miraculous.

I'd gone to see him for issues with urination, bowel management and sexual function. Fortunately Dr. Johnson helped me understand the possible steps to take to create a sense of normalcy in my life. We started with self-catheterization.

I figure I've catheterized myself close to 25,000 times since then. It was tough in the beginning learning how to insert the small, sterile tube into the head of my penis, through my urethra, and into my bladder to drain the urine. The only instruction I had gotten was a CD that came with my first shipment of catheters.

He warned me about the constant risk of infection. With no sensation, a urinary tract infection (UTI) can be rampant before I'm even aware of it. It's a daily risk.

But I've discovered that the greater challenge with the catheters has to do with managing them. You can't just go into a store and buy as many as you want. They're dispensed in limited numbers, on a prescription-only basis, and closely monitored by the insurance company that pays for them. It's not enough to ask the supplier to refill my prescription: it has to be regularly reviewed—even though due to my spinal cord injury the condition of my bladder will never change—and approved before catheters can be shipped. It feels like trying to get permission from a bank for an interest-free loan. And I have to go through the review process every three months.

Whenever our travel plans overlap with a foreseeable need for more catheters, the stress level ratchets up since no one at the supplier's end seems to be accountable. One false promise after another, combined often with a liberal dose of incompetence, and we find ourselves down to the last minute. More often than not, it seems like a comedy of errors but it's not the slightest bit funny.

I remember one time in particular when we were getting ready to leave for Hawaii. Despite having put the ball in motion well in advance, approval of the paperwork took longer than anticipated but finally we had confirmation from the supplier that the catheters would be delivered the day before our departure. I would stay home all day in order to receive the delivery since there was no way of knowing what time the courier would arrive.

While I was having coffee in the morning I heard a vehicle on the street. I got up and looked out the window. It was our neighbor's landscaper pulling up for his regular maintenance. Several hours later while I was collecting the mail, I saw a UPS truck turn into our street. I stood up a little straighter, alert and ready to accept the box containing a three-month supply of catheters from the driver. The truck stopped at the house two doors up. By mid afternoon I was becoming frantic.

At 3 p.m. I called the supplier. "We turned the package over to the courier, and the computer says they'll deliver today. Sorry, there's nothing more we can do." A call to the courier was much the same. "According to the computer, you should receive the package today. The driver is in your area."

Our flight was scheduled to leave early the following day. We considered our options: change our flight, request delivery to where we'd be staying in Hawaii (adding three extra days for delivery), or get down on our knees and pray. None of our options could guarantee I'd have the catheters in hand when I needed them.

In emergencies I have to "double up", in other words use the same catheter twice. It's risky because even the slightest contamination can mean setting off a dreaded urinary tract infection, which can quickly start flowing through my system unhindered, causing permanent damage, sometimes requiring dialysis or a kidney transplant. I *always* keep a supply of antibiotics on hand in case I get that unmistakable smell from my urine. When I think I might have a problem, I literally stick my nose into the toilet just to make sure I'm okay.

Jill and I have been known to tear through every gym bag, suitcase, purse, closet, backpack, and car glove box like crazed demons to find where we might have stashed an extra one or two catheters so I can get through another day until delivery.

This particular time, right at the last minute, when we were about to call the airline to change our flight, the courier pulled up in front of the house. For a second, panic struck: maybe the package the driver had for us was something else entirely, maybe he didn't have the catheters. I bolted out the front door. "Hey, I thought you'd never get here," I said with a nervous chuckle, trying to make light of the situation.

"Last delivery of the day!" the driver smiled as he handed over the familiar box. Finally, I could breathe easily.

Through it all, I've learned to be scrupulous about hygiene and well-organized regarding supplies. (I can proudly say that I've only had two UTIs out of the tens of thousands of times I've used a catheter—not bad stats!) Taking care of a body with a spinal cord injury can involve uncomfortable and often unpleasant details but keeping a compromised body in working order is a must.

Dealing with challenges doesn't necessarily mean liking them. I never liked making cold calls and it took me a very long time to come to terms with relying on a catheter, but by getting comfortable with being uncomfortable I overcame the anxiety those situations once caused.

FOUR

IT'S A SLOW DRIP

Throughout my ordeal, my desire to improve and get stronger hasn't faded but at the same time I've had a hidden fear of setting myself up for disappointment. With previous injuries and surgeries, I'd set and accomplished the goal of returning my body to the level of fitness and mobility I'd had before. With the spinal cord injury, I spent the first couple of years trying to get my head fully around the brutal fact that this time was different. My old self effectively died on December 30, 2008—how could I or would I ever accept that? My glass was half empty, and I suspected that if I ever saw it as half full again I'd have to pass through hell first. I was already suffering physically and mentally and the thought of adding disappointment to the mix was scary. I was barely holding on. If I started to feel that I'd let myself down, I wasn't sure I'd make it.

There's never been a morning when I woke up and said, "Ah, it's a miracle, I can feel my feet!" or "Wow, I've got sensation between my legs!" I've never experienced an improvement of that sort, where one day I could suddenly do something that had been impossible the day before. My guess is that it's pretty much the norm for anyone who is dealing with overwhelming physical or emotional trauma.

I wish I'd understood better just how drawn-out the healing process can be. And I wish I'd understood that nobody can predict accurately to what degree an individual may recover after an injury. There's no set finish line like in a marathon, no final buzzer at the end of four quarters. In my case, eleven years after my accident, I'm still recovering, discovering improvements and changes that tell me my nerves are regenerating in small ways.

Toward the end of 2009, when I was psychologically at one of my lowest points, I kept hearing—from surgeons and other people who treat spinal cord injuries like mine—that whatever recovery you're going to get will take place within the first twelve to eighteen months following your accident. After that, you've got what you've got. Those words—*you've got what you've got*—rang in my ears.

Like many people with a spinal cord injury, depression was constantly lurking and frequently elbowed its way through the door until finally it was front and center, forcing me to surrender to its demands. As I neared the twelve-month mark, the effects of my nerve damage, pain, and weakness seemed to be worsening rather than improving. That message, *you've got what you've got,* added to my deepening depression.

Frequent episodes of neuropathic pain and weakness in my lower body frightened me to my core. Living with those sensations until the end of my natural life would be tortuous. Often, when I felt the impulses surge, I would ease my wasted body onto the recliner in our family room, close my eyes, and just try to survive.

I remember one Sunday when my family decided to go out to brunch; I couldn't rise from the recliner to join them. After they left, I moaned and cried and sobbed. Even though it was a weekend, I called my doctor's office in total desperation, knowing that no one would answer the phone but unable to resist the urge to beg for help. I felt locked in the prison of my pain.

One day, I wrote to my physiatrist, a specialist who assists patients with paralysis, severe nerve damage and spinal cord-injury issues: *I can feel the tidal wave coming. I've taken a whole Percocet and it doesn't even dent the pain. I can't imagine anything worse, I just can't.*

If this was what I got, how could I live with it? When each day brought me to my knees, exhausted by the sheer effort of dealing with the blinding pain, where in God's name would I find the strength to go on? How can a man feel like a man when he has to wear a diaper and has no hope of ever making love to his wife again? I can tell you, he doesn't.

Fortunately, not all doctors ascribe to the you've-got-what-you've-got concept. There are some who treat people over long periods of time, who focus on the continuum and have seen recoveries that were not expected. I was lucky enough to have two physicians of this type in my corner.

When I informed New York Life about my accident, the company put me in contact with Dr. John Roglieri. "He's available to you if you need assistance," the email said.

An internist who has treated many of the company's big executives, he's a "tough love" kind of doctor and when I told him about the you've-got-what-you've-got scenario he reminded me that nobody's all right or all wrong. The surgeon's first call immediately after my accident was that I'd be confined to a wheelchair and, as Dr. Roglieri explained, that was the right call for the type of burst fracture and other injuries I sustained. "But how right were the doctors about *you*? About your willpower and never-say-die attitude? Were they aware of your fitness before the accident or your prior recoveries from setbacks? Did they have the tools to assess your faith that recovery is possible? Continue hearing them out, then set your own most likely scenario and keep modifying it as things develop," he said.

I took his words of wisdom to heart, but that didn't get me off the most formidable emotional roller coaster imaginable. I wrote in my journal: *How can it happen that one week I have my very best day since the injury and then get crushed under the darkness of brutal pain and depression only days later? It is impossible to describe how discouraging it is to know that in a heartbeat I can regress.* Pushed and pulled between understanding the process, being patient and keeping focused, and full-blown clinical depression was exhausting. More than once, Dr. Roglieri talked me down off the edge of the cliff.

Another doctor who was instrumental in helping me pull through was physiatrist Dr. Elaine Date. When we first met she told me that among many of her patients she'd witnessed amazing recoveries, all of which took a long time to unfold. She monitored my progress for approximately four years, keeping detailed notes about changes in my sensitivity and strength. She'd take a needle, then start at my feet and poke. "Can you feel this?" Up, up, and up my body she would continue, covering each and every part. She kept telling me, "You're going to come out of this. You've just got to hang in there." Having a person with her experience reassuring me was so important.

In addition, I partnered with a personal trainer named Michaela Lien. She had expertise in working on the inner girdle of muscle fibers that wrap around a person's core, where I had the titanium cage encasing my spine. I knew from my experience after the staph infection that those muscles were the ones to target first and I'm glad I chose to work with her because if I'd tried rehabbing on my own, I would most likely have done too much too soon and risked hurting myself. That old desire of mine to overachieve was lurking beneath the surface and for once in my life I approached my physical challenges with moderation and good sense rather than charging forward, crashing into whatever obstacle that was in my way.

I also got a recommendation for a massage therapist. I wanted to give my body the greatest chance for recovery and regain at least some of the sensation I'd lost. It was very slow going in the beginning because my broken body had become so used to holding onto its pain that I could barely stand being touched.

Ben Cabal is a highly skilled professional and in his finely-tuned hands each part of my body eventually yielded to the necessary kneading and prodding. His fingers, forearms, shoulders and legs penetrated every nook and cranny of my entire body to coerce the trauma out of my cells. It wasn't the sort of relaxing massage you get at a spa, that's for sure, but it was what I needed.

If you really think about how long it actually takes for you to completely heal after you've cut your finger, for example—to the point where there's no heightened sensitivity or hint of a scar—it's kind of crazy to expect a body subjected to a spinal cord injury to complete its full arc of recovery within the space of a year and a half.

After certain traumas some people can never return to their pre-trauma condition, sometimes it's just not possible. But that doesn't mean there's no recovery.

From my experience, recovery doesn't gush like a fully opened spigot. It's a slow drip. Anyone who's put a pot under a ceiling leak knows, as long as the drip persists the pot continues to fill. When the depression receded into the background, I tried to focus on that drip. *Plink. Plink. Plink.* I don't think the people I interacted with on a daily basis were aware of the drip, but those who saw me once every year or two always commented on my progress.

With my earlier sports-related injuries and surgeries there were doctors who told me I'd be good as new after six months. Well, that was rarely the case, it was more like a year. So if it took my younger body a year for something much less, wouldn't it take a lot longer to recover after what I'd gone through?

Neither of these concepts of recovery time—six months after a "routine" surgery and a maximum of twelve to eighteen months after a spinal cord injury with not much change afterwards—fit with what I felt in my gut, or with what I had experienced. Doctors didn't know my ability to persevere, they didn't understand how stubborn I can be about doing one set to exhaustion. They were experts on the human body, but not *my* body, I kept reminding myself.

I was coming to grips with the fact that I would never be the same, but I worked at recovery as if I had a chance to, getting truly comfortable being uncomfortable. There were days when all I could do was walk up the stairs but, damn it, I was going to walk up them as fast as I possibly could on that day. I was going to push myself—one set to exhaustion—each and every day in my pursuit of full recovery, no matter what the doctors said. If I was able to look myself in the mirror at the end of the day and say, "Today, I did the very best I could," then I knew I was making progress. It was a matter of accountability, to *myself*. That best effort and accountability helped carry me through the hopelessness and despair.

Consider a team that's behind. If the players give up because they believe they have no chance of winning, a loss is guaranteed. I'm not willing to accept a loss without a fight. Over the past eleven years I've been fighting, and continue to fight, to gain whatever yardage I can.

It's important to remember, though, that everybody's different. How each person's recovery progresses will be just as individual as they are, and as singular as the factors surrounding the adversity.

The first factor that sets the tempo for recovery is the seriousness of the setback: a person's time to heal is directly related to the gravity of the insult. The tendinitis in my elbow formed over a span of years, so it's logical that it took a prolonged period of time to recover. Another factor is age. Wounds generally heal more slowly as a person ages. Scientists tell us that, among other things, special white blood cells called macrophages are critical in regenerating connective tissue and collagen, and aging interferes with interactions between these and stem cells.

Another reason has to do with inflammation, which is an important part of the healing puzzle. As a person ages they tend to have more inflammatory cells circulating and this can lead to impaired recovery. These are aspects outside a person's control. In this regard, it's true that you've got what you've got.

Then there are factors that a person *can* control. I can't emphasize enough how important it is to prepare for adversity and commit to being as healthy as possible before a setback. I've seen countless men and women in the gym in their 60s, 70s, and even 80s, who have been bitten by the weight-training bug. Personally I've found building functional strength addictive and once you feel your body working for you, you'll never want to lose it. The difference between doing something and doing nothing can be life-changing.

Another key, controllable aspect is compliance with the prescribed therapy. If medications are indicated, take them. If you need to do specific exercises, do them. You can't expect to improve if you don't do what you're supposed to. I'm not saying it's easy to always do what will move you toward recovery but commitment to the goal is a first step.

Your healing environment is critical as well. I was lucky enough to live on a quiet street and not have any barriers between my house and the sidewalk. Even on the days when I felt raw and unable to face the world, I could safely get out for a walk. The support of my family meant I could focus on improving without major distractions. Choosing the right people to have around you while you're fighting to get better is essential. And don't ever underestimate the power of laughter and humor.

In early summer 2009, Jill's brother came to live with us for a while. He was going through a divorce and needed a place to regroup. Our spare bedroom was available so it seemed logical for him to move in. One evening as we sat around the table after dinner, he said, referring to our address, "This isn't Rose Lane, this is Adversity Lane!" Hell, I was a mess from my accident and additional surgery, he was in the middle of a difficult divorce, and Joey had dropped out of college and felt lost without baseball. We were quite a trio.

After a moment's pause when we each considered silently whether what he'd said was funny or pathetic, the three of us started laughing. Roaring with laughter, pounding the table with laughter, tears rolling from our eyes laughter. It was the first time I'd really cut loose since the accident and it felt great. Every night for several weeks the three of us would huddle around the table and make each other laugh.

I swear, it was some of the most effective medicine I've ever taken. It was free and had no nasty side effects!

Preparing and sharing food with people I care about has also been a sort of holistic medicine. For years, it's been one of my favorite ways to unwind. I love shopping for fresh ingredients, chopping vegetables and herbs, choosing the right wine, tossing something out of the ordinary into the simmering pot or tending to meat as it sizzles on the grill. Everyone knows that sharing a meal is a simple pleasure that brings people together. Discovering that I could still turn on a food processor, fire up a barbecue, shop and offer nourishment to others was a triumph. Especially in light of my struggle to stay, let's say, on the playing field.

My friend Mike Piotrowicz and I are linked, in part, by a shared passion for the pleasures of the kitchen. In his own special way, he reminded me that all was not lost. And he didn't waste any time about it.

Mike has been an amazing mentor for me in my business, but first and foremost we are dear friends. Everyone knows that true friendship is hard to come by, especially when it's a relationship established later in life, but I can say we literally fell in love with each other when we first met, and so did our families.

Before I was even out of the rehab center in Reno, Mike announced, "We need to cook together. What do you want to make for these people?"

At first, I was skeptical. I'd barely reacquired the confidence to stand upright, could I really think about cooking? But in his wisdom, Mike knew that getting me in front of a stove would provide me with a much-needed boost.

"How about some chicken, tomato and basil risotto?" It was a recipe I'd made hundreds of times, and always to the delight of whoever I shared it with. The folks at the rehab center had no idea what was coming their way!

Besides the diversion and pleasure cooking offered, Mike's idea gave me the chance for my first outing: a trip to the grocery store. Feasting my eyes on the fresh produce and imagining the flavors and aromas of a gourmet dish lifted my spirits as much as any of the other accomplishments I'd achieved. Maybe life after a spinal cord injury really was possible.

Back at the rehab center, it didn't take long before the promising scent of simmering onions and chicken broth wafted through the corridors. As Jill wrote in an email, *Lots of happy staff, nurses, patients, and construction workers at St. Mary's rehab. Everyone got a serving of Bill's famous chicken, tomato and basil risotto and none of them were disappointed. Bill had a great time working his magic on the stovetop. The halls of the 4th floor never smelled so good!*

In the subsequent weeks, months and even years, cooking acted as a bridge from despair toward some sort of happiness. So what if my mobility was affected? I could still dream up new recipes, whip ingredients into flavorful dishes and share my passion for food with the people I love. That lunch Mike and I made at the hospital reminded me that I hadn't lost everything, some pleasures were still available to me despite the loss of others. I could choose to participate in life.

Being able to get in a car and drive where I wanted symbolized, in another way, participating in life. It suggested independence and freedom.

When I first came home from the hospital, driving a car was physically impossible and, honestly, not even something I thought about. I was terribly uncomfortable in a car and my feeling of being vulnerable in a moving vehicle was mammoth. What would happen if another car hit us? It seemed that whenever Jill and I went somewhere I'd scream at her, "Don't hit the damn pothole!" "Watch out!" If I was feeling brutalized by the pain and dread, I can only imagine how horrible she must have felt. The agony that bumps, turns, and quick stops provoked was torture and being a passenger meant being totally helpless.

As I slowly made progress physically, however, the desire for the freedom that driving represented bubbled to the surface. Besides, I told myself, Jill had her life to live and I didn't want to weigh on her any more than I already was. I was afraid of being a burden and yearned for independence although navigating the fine line between asking for or accepting help and doing things for myself was another challenge. I can look back now and recognize that I didn't always succeed. However, I instinctively knew that the time had come to get out and do things on my own.

I spent hours lounging in a recliner at home during my convalescence, Chipper stretched out on the hardwood floor beside me, as I maintained contact by phone with clients and instructed my support staff in the office. I did what I could but for three years after my injury I had to lean heavily on my team. The star player is my amazing assistant Julie Ortega. She's worked with me for almost thirty-five years and, having witnessed me interacting with clients and attended so many meetings, we joke that she knows what I'm about to say before the words even leave my mouth. She kept the ball moving on the field while I was sidelined, but there came the time when I needed to physically get back in the game.

I started off by going into the office for just an hour or so, as a way to have some face-to-face interaction, as a distraction, a way to defeat the boredom. Despite the physical pain and the embarrassment about my appearance, going to my workplace ended up being a total life-saver. But asking Jill to drive me such a short distance left me feeling like I was interrupting her plans and forcing her to organize her day around what I wanted. Hell, it wasn't far, and my body was responding to therapy. I could drive myself. Besides, I wanted to be certain that I didn't hinder my recovery by being too dependent, a risk that often lurks in the shadows of fear.

I approached driving again like I had approached everything else in my life. It was something that I thought needed to be done and therefore I did it. I barreled forward like when I was a high school football player—probably not the wisest thing to do but it was the only thing I knew how to do at the time. Fortunately, I didn't have or (knowingly) cause any accidents but looking back, I probably should have waited longer before getting behind the wheel. Due to the meds, I didn't always recognize traffic issues quickly and it was scary not being able to feel the pedals with my feet. Foolishly, I didn't consider the potential consequences; I was focused exclusively on re-joining the rest of the world and avoiding depression.

Driving was no different from being the passenger: irregularities in the road sent me through the roof from a pain standpoint. And while I didn't really feel at ease driving, the idea of calling a friend or colleague and asking for a ride didn't even occur to me—a stupid guy thing, as if asking for help means you're not really a man. What BS.

Later, when I received that bright, shiny blue, permanent placard with the symbol of a wheelchair embossed on it, I had to accept that I was truly disabled. The State of California said so. The reality was that I desperately needed the designation. Even just getting into and out of my car required a Herculean effort, while getting from the car to a store, office or restaurant—even though I could park right in front—often taxed my energy to the point where I was running on empty.

In the beginning, I agreed to only drive to the office, a three-minute jaunt from home. As the months passed, I ventured farther and I remember driving myself to some of my medical appointments on the other side of the Bay. I also remember having some close calls in traffic, and fighting to keep my focus on the road and calm my jittering hands after the danger had passed.

I continued going to my office for a couple of hours at a time for several years, never working anything close to a full day. Having that freedom to pop in briefly, to hang out with people I knew well whose attention did not focus on my physical predicament, and to keep the mental wheels turning were huge benefits that helped keep the depression monster at bay.

To say, even now, that I'm fully comfortable driving would be a lie. My hands grip the steering wheel at ten and two, just like the driving instructor tells you when you first start out. I'm also especially careful about the shoes I wear. Never sandals or any sort of footwear that might slip or impede my contact with the pedals. I'm constantly vigilant: somebody could run a red light and I'd have to start this recovery business all over again.

Another destination I could easily drive to was my local gym.

I've gone to the same one for years and I recently discovered that they keep records of attendance. I had the opportunity to review mine from October 2006 to June 2019: a total of about 1200 visits to the gym, with approximately half of them logged after my accident. There's a noticeable gap between December 29, 2008 and February 21, 2009 since I obviously couldn't go while I was in the hospital. But I was back in the gym just two and a half weeks after I got home, less than two months after my accident. Exercising my muscles was the only thing I could think of doing, although in hindsight, I'm surprised I was back in the gym so quickly in light of the amount of pain I was in.

I did my exercises in the upstairs room where the weight machines are located and an important part of my training was climbing those stairs. In fact, climbing stairs, whether it was at home, at the gym or at my office, was instrumental in my rehabilitation. I've never liked to take the easy way or ask for help and I do believe that this has played to my favor.

A good part of my routine required floor work. Exercises to strengthen the inner core muscles that I'd learned when I was recovering from the staph infection. Small, controlled, Pilates-type movements to reconstruct the lower abdominal, back and oblique muscles. When I'd done them religiously to recover from the infection, I built a complex of muscles wrapping around my lower torso that was stronger than I'd ever experienced. My aim now was to re-acquire that muscle tone.

Getting down onto the floor didn't really pose a problem but, in the beginning, I was too weak to get back on my feet. I had to crawl to the railing and slowly pull myself up—another opportunity to work my muscles.

Reviewing those attendance records, I noticed that in the year prior to my accident I'd gone to the gym approximately 200 times, and the year before even more. This translates to consistent attendance at least every other day and sometimes every day. Here was evidence that the medical staff had been right about my fitness level leading into the trauma—I'd been in excellent shape. It's likely that by staying fit, I'd kept myself out of a wheelchair, and maybe it even saved my life.

In the initial post-accident years, of course the frequency of my gym attendance was greatly reduced but there is a huge difference between no visits and a modest number of visits. My friend Dr. King reminds me that, for everyone, building functional strength is essential as we age. Like the current in a river that carries you downstream, aging propels you toward a final, inevitable destination. The alternative is to swim against the current. It's true that, in the end, you can't avoid that destination but by continuing to swim you can improve the quality of your daily life.

As the months passed, my physical body began to shed the trauma. Not like a snake that leaves its nearly intact skin lying on the hard desert floor, but rather cell by cell in tiny increments that no one can actually see. Oftentimes not even I was aware of the progress, overcome as I was by the neuropathic pain and the exhaustion of trying to get through each day. But the fact is, I was consistently working toward my recovery. There were some days when the best I could do was tell myself to just focus on getting through until tomorrow. And when I was feeling really overwhelmed, I'd break whatever obstacle was in front of me into even smaller segments. Like I did on the football field, focusing on making a first down rather than aiming for the goal line. Had I turned my eyes toward the final objective too soon, I fear I would have given up.

I believe that everyone—no matter how they approach a trauma—has the seeds of recovery lying dormant inside them, ready to sprout given the right conditions. In my case, the seeds had a number of opportunities to germinate over the years and so I was maybe better prepared for what I was facing. Someone else may have to dig extra deep, but those seeds *are* there. To find your own example of tapping into their energy, think of a time when you looked back and said to yourself, "Wow, I never thought

I could do that," after having taken on a seemingly insurmountable challenge. That feeling of overachievement, of pride in your accomplishment that makes you stand a little taller are external manifestations of that energy.

FIVE

PAIN TRUMPS EVERYTHING

I'm convinced there is no human being who can win when it comes to fighting brutal, 24/7 chronic pain. I'm not talking here about the dull discomfort a person learns to live with or the occasional stab of pain that makes you grit your teeth and blocks the air in your lungs. What I'm talking about is mind-blowing pain that sucks every ounce of force out of a body, that demands full attention and precludes thought or movement, constantly.

In a healthy person, nerves transmit information to the brain, via the spinal cord, about what's happening to the body and the brain sends back impulses telling the body what to do in reaction. For example, when I tore the anterior cruciate ligament in my left knee while playing college football, I felt pain because the tissues suffered damage and my brain sent the impulse of pain which effectively told me to stay still so that I wouldn't damage it further. This is an example of acute pain.

Chronic pain, on the other hand, results when pain receptors keep sending impulses, usually because there's still tissue damage but sometimes even if the injury has healed. There are many people who suffer from chronic back pain, for example. Neuropathic pain, which is caused by nerve damage or disease of the nervous system, is one type of chronic pain. Furthermore, there are different types of nerve fibers in the body and they transmit different types of sensations, as well as other types of pain. And pain signals travel through regions of the brain that govern emotions and thinking, so psychological, emotional and social factors are involved too.

Conversely, under high stress conditions, people with severe injuries may experience no pain, for example soldiers in combat who have a severe wound but keep fighting and discover it later, or parents who've sustained life-threatening injuries but free their children from the wreckage of an accident.

All of this means that pain, which is regulated by the mind, can be difficult to manage.

The pain that's frequently part of a spinal cord injury is particularly complex. Even if a certain part of your body no longer has sensation, the signals that damaged nerves send to your brain get misunderstood and you experience very real, often excruciating pain emanating from that site.

Perhaps because I had already dealt with chronic pain over the years due to my sports-related injuries and surgeries, I thought I could handle the pain that comes with a spinal cord injury. I was wrong. One way I describe what I experienced, and continue to experience today, is terribly brutal but it's accurate. It's the sensation of having a glass Coke bottle, with its neck broken off and heated until it's glowing orange, shoved into my rectum. What fluctuates is my perception of how big, how hot, or how sharp the bottle is. In addition, since I have no sensation in my butt cheeks, whenever I sit down, no matter what sort of cushion there is, it feels like I'm sitting on a pile of rocks. For years, my calves have felt as if they're wrapped tightly with duct tape. And when I walk, it feels as if a very strong man is holding me back, his huge hands squeezing each butt cheek to keep me from moving forward. Then there's the sensation of a rope being twisted upward around my genitals and inner thighs. Trust me, a person can't make this stuff up. These are real attempts to describe what I feel. I've also got varying degrees of numbness and burning sensations that have at times been compounded by bouts of spasticity in my legs, as well as the psychological torture of bladder and bowel dysfunction and loss of sexual function.

For a previously active and physically-fit fifty-two year old man, the incontinence was devastating. I did however receive a side benefit from the bladder dysfunction. Having a neurogenic bladder means that I also have a lack of feeling regarding the natural urge to urinate. Most middle-aged men get the urge too often in the middle of the night, instead I have hours of glorious uninterrupted sleep. I do believe this bit of silver lining has aided my recovery.

About nine months after my accident, I began searching on the internet to find someone or some group of people who'd had a similar trauma or were dealing with similar symptoms. Unfortunately, I didn't find much and it only reinforced my feelings of helplessness.

Deep down I didn't really expect to find another person just like me who'd gone through what I was experiencing, but I was looking for some reassurance. I felt alone and on my own, without a roadmap. All I could do was rely on the foundation of persistence and perseverance that was wired into my DNA. I figured I'd tough it out but the constant, unrelenting, gut-wrenching physical and emotional pain took its toll. Pain of that degree breaks everybody down at some point in time. That's the nature of the beast.

So, on the one hand I was fortunate enough to have this inner strength that urged me on but, on the other, the raw power of violent pain, the side effects of all the drugs, and the humiliation of pissing and shitting my pants were grinding me into the dirt.

Around the same time, I sent a message to my sons. Sending messages to all three of them at the same time was one way to make sure everyone knew what was going on, especially since they weren't around for the day-to-day.

Joe had moved to Santa Barbara to finish up his degree at the University of California. Bret was a student at the University of Pennsylvania. Fortunately he'd been home for the holidays when I had my accident, but his return to school was hard on all of us, especially since he was so far away. Craig got the brunt of the immediate trauma since he was with me when I fell. The sorrow I still feel about what he had to witness on the Nightmare run remains indelible but I thank God that he was with me. Who knows what would have happened if I had been alone.

I wrote the message to the boys after Jill and I came home from a dinner with friends to celebrate her fifty-first birthday. I'd been struggling with finding the right balance between pain meds and their effects, including severe constipation. I was trying to counteract the problem with laxatives but was losing the battle. That evening had been particularly frustrating and messy. *I can't tell you how many pairs of underwear I've thrown away in various places over the last nine months*, I wrote. It was an uncomfortable confession to make and, while I didn't relay the details, I'd repeated the same experience probably a hundred times in those previous 270 days. *I can't stand the pain without the meds. This next month has to be better. I don't think I can get any worse, but I've said that before. Whatever comes my way, I will not give up fighting.*

Unfortunately, several months later, things did go from bad to worse and it seemed that all we could do was grasp at straws. The nerve pain was unbearable and, with all the rest, I was at my wits' end.

I was straying toward the other side of the line that separates wanting to live from not wanting to live. When the pain was brutal, I doubted my ability to get over to the other side, to be in a place where I wanted to live and not die. I wasn't expecting to be pain-free—the doctors had made it clear they predicted that as an impossibility—I just knew that there was an amount of pain I could tolerate long-term and an amount that I couldn't.

I can only imagine that having to watch the person you love experience constant pain was equally hard. Jill is one of the strongest people I know and even she broke down in tears one evening at our friends' house in front of three other couples. I'd never seen her reveal her emotions so openly before. I hated being the one to put her through all of it but I was helpless.

That very sense of helplessness eventually began to impact our marriage, at least it did from my side. Jill bravely faced each day as it came and maintained a we'll-worry-about-tomorrow-when-tomorrow-comes attitude, but I had a loop in my head that her life would improve if I was out of the way. *Probably better we part company amicably, no need for you to hang with damaged goods. You're a young 51 with a lot of life left to live and I'm not going to take that away from you,* I wrote in a message to her while we sat in a room full of elegantly dressed men and women at a gala fundraiser.

Her reply: *Screw you.*

Text messages and hand-written notes were frequent between us as we tried to cope. A spoken conversation was impossible to control, and therefore frightening. Overwhelming emotion was constantly threatening to escape from inside the closed container of a brain or a heart. We both knew it was essential to communicate but neither of us had processed our own emotions sufficiently to deal with those of the other. Our verbal exchanges were largely limited to the basics of the day-to-day—medications, catheters, food, sleep.

If it weren't for Jill's fierce, constant presence and unwavering support, I don't know if we would have survived as a couple. To be perfectly clear, I deserve none, absolutely zero of the credit for our staying together. Under the constant assault of mind-bending, incomprehensible pain I wasn't capable of understanding the depth and strength of my wife's love for me and our family.

Time and again, I lashed out at those I love in a terribly mean, mean way and I'll regret my hateful words and actions for the rest of my life. Thank God Jill didn't listen to the stupid stuff that came out of my mouth and understood it wasn't really me talking.

For anyone who finds themselves facing a situation similar to mine: expect the relationship with your partner to be tested. Remember that your relationship isn't the problem, it's your setback that's causing the friction. You're in pain and unable to think things through or make decisions. You're most likely reacting to the moment. Exhaustion has worn down your nerves till they're raw and chafed. Sometimes just taking one more breath can feel like too much.

Each time I handed a new physician or therapist my file, there was silence as they absorbed the recorded facts. Then they'd lift their head and say something like, "My God, that's a horrible accident you had. I can't believe you're walking." I'd make some comment and they'd go back to reviewing the file and the second thing they'd say was, "Are you still married?" Those four words say volumes about the impact serious adversity can have on a couple.

In mid-November, about ten and a half months after my accident, the constant physical and emotional pain had totally broken me down. The idea of suicide became part of my daily thoughts. I had been doing my best to deal with the clinical depression that often follows a spinal cord injury but I was slipping, losing my grip. While the realization now of how close I came to losing it is frightening, it's not surprising. Estimated rates of severe depression for people with a spinal cord injury go as high as almost 40%, while they hover around 7% among the general adult population.

Even though I was determined to fight with all I had, the lack of a clear way forward clouded my reasoning more and more. A perfect example of my mixed state of mind comes from a get well card I received in that period. On the front there was this quote from Winston Churchill: *If you're going through hell, keep going.* The sender of the card had chosen a message he knew would touch me, and it did. But on the back of the card I scrawled, *It's Sunday November 22, 2009. I couldn't be more miserable or depressed. I have paid a huge price to be able to walk but I will keep fighting until I die. I won't stop no matter how brutal the pain becomes. Avoiding a wheelchair is worth every second of misery. However, no human being can continue to exist in my state.* My words reflect how resolute I was about retaining my mobility but at the same time they reveal that I knew I couldn't hold on much longer. The fatigue of hitting my head against the wall was breaking my will.

I talked myself into believing that my family would be fine without me. My financial planning was in place, not only for the immediate term but also for after I was gone, and I thought that was the extent of what they needed.

Three days later I wrote to my two best friends, Warren and Mike. I have immense respect for both of these men and felt compelled to share with them where I was mentally. I explained that my doctors had come to the conclusion they couldn't position a pump in my back to deliver targeted pain-relief medication due to my prior surgeries. Instead, they were attempting to combine various tricyclic drugs and a long-lasting opioid to help me deal with the pain but the idea of flooding my body with even more powerful drugs terrified me. I imagined being turned into some sort of zombie. *People say, 'focus on what you have,' I wrote. Well, 80% of what I used to have is gone and as for the other 20%, I won't know what's going on when I have it. I can't even piss, shit, have sex, exercise, work, focus or think clearly now.*

I think if someone had told me at that point that I had a terminal brain tumor and would be dead in six months, I would have said, "Great, bring it on."

I needed to know if there was a chance of getting back onto the other side of that suicide line, to a place where I wanted to live and not die. Was there reason to hope? From where I stood I couldn't find an answer, and it was destroying me.

After I sent the email, I called Warren. "I think I'm gonna commit suicide."

Warren had challenged me at tetherball on the playground when we were seven years old. He was the new kid at school and I was the undisputed tetherball champion. He beat the pants off me and we've been like brothers ever since.

When we were at college together, he was my academic role model and while our studies led him to become an orthopedic surgeon and carried me toward financial planning, we share a strong work ethic and have always turned to each other for professional expertise. When I started having sports injuries, I went to Warren. He's operated on my shoulders, knees, and elbows. It's incredibly reassuring to look up at your best-friend doctor, who has worked in some of the toughest hospitals around as well as operated on some of the highest profile athletes, while you're lying on the operating table waiting for the anesthesia to take over. Knowing that you're in his hands banishes all negative thoughts.

I called him that day looking for the same unemotional, matter-of-fact steadiness I'd witnessed in the operating room. I couldn't find it in myself and hoped he had enough of it for me too.

"Well," he said calmly while pondering my suicide comment, "that's an option and it might be the best one for you but I can tell you almost for sure it's not the best option for your family. Jill and the boys would be devastated."

Hmm, I hadn't thought of that. I was sure they'd be taken care of financially, I thought that was enough.

I'd planned the whole thing. How I would walk to the end of my cul-de-sac and up into the hills. How I would call the police and tell them where I was and that I would be dead when they arrived. And how I would actually do it.

The only type of guns I owned were shotguns for shooting game birds. I used to go hunting with my brothers, Warren and other friends out in the scrubby Nevada sagebrush for quail and chukar, an occasional sage hen. Quality guy-time with our dogs when we could cut loose and celebrate male bonding.

I went into the garage one day when I was alone. I couldn't imagine ever being able to go hunting with my buddies again, but I did have something else in mind. I unlocked the case where I kept my shotguns. I considered the length of the barrel on each. I chose the shortest one. I took the gun out of its case and admired its configuration, the efficiency of each part, how it was perfectly designed for its intended purpose. I felt its heft, pausing on how the stock carries the majority of the weight. I thought back to the last time I'd used it—I had hit my target. A male pheasant as it lifted from the brush, the sound of its flapping wings impossible to ignore in the morning silence. One single shot, swift, clean, painless I hoped.

If I followed through on what I was thinking of doing with that gun, there could be no mistakes. Standing there, with the gun in my hands reassured me—there was no reason to believe my weapon would let me down.

The rules of gun safety are drilled into the mind of every conscientious person who owns a firearm: 1) assume that all guns are loaded; 2) never let the muzzle of the gun cover anything you're not willing to destroy; 3) keep your finger off the trigger until you've made the decision to shoot; 4) be sure of your target and what lies beyond it.

Confirming that the chamber was empty, I turned the shotgun around so the barrel was facing me. It was an unnatural action, something like how getting behind the wheel of a car, putting on a blindfold and turning the ignition must feel. I opened my mouth and put the barrel in as far as I could. It was cold on my lips, its metallic taste oddly comforting. I extended my right arm and set my thumb on the trigger. It was an easy reach.

So, now I knew the how and I'd already figured out the where. It was just a question of when.

I must have gone over each step in my head fifty, a hundred times as I laid in my bed, the fire of the spastic contractions grabbing at my butt muscles, the imagined Coke bottle stabbing inside me, the sensation of a blunt object being shoved into my penis forcing me to contort against my will. I prayed that something would pull me back from the edge before I said to hell with it all.

I've kept the journal I wrote in during that time, as well as all the cards and notes I received, and have also found some that I wrote. I still have a piece of paper pulled from a small notepad. There's an image of a golfer at the bottom next to the symbol of the United States Golf Association. There's no mistaking I wrote the message, the uneasy flow of printed letters are mine for sure. Reading it now is bone-chilling, but that was my state of mind.

Do you think I should tell the kids I am going to kill myself or should I just do it without disclosure. No answer means it is up to me.

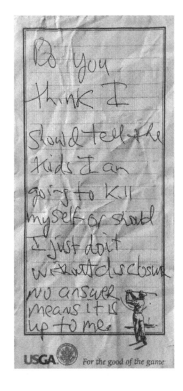

Note to my wife, mid 2010.

Due to where my spine was injured, I no longer have sexual function or sensation. That means no erections and no orgasms. No reaction to touch or contact. I saw it as being stripped of my manhood. I was bitter and angry.

Just before the accident, Jill and I had been experiencing a rebirth in our marriage. The stresses and struggles that couples go through while raising a family had been, for the most part, put behind us and we were rediscovering and falling in love with each other all over again. Ironically, it made me feel the loss even more deeply.

I have a very clear memory of an evening in early 2010. I'd recently been diagnosed as clinically depressed and had started taking Cymbalta and Wellbutrin. Jill and I were up in the bedroom, attempting to create some intimacy, some physical connection that could provide momentary pleasure to counteract the anguish of our reality. But it's almost impossible to want to be touched or have the focus to give pleasure to your partner when you feel like a hot, sharp instrument is being shoved into you from behind. Exhausted from trying, I started to cry. "We're fucked," I mumbled and Jill pulled me closer. Together our tears flowed and flowed, seemingly without end like our despair. We mourned for what appeared to be the total demise of our intimate relationship.

Once I'd recovered physically enough to travel, we took a trip with our closest friends. One evening, while sharing another wonderful dinner together after a full day enjoying each other's company, the language of love was in full play between the other four couples, but not for Jill and I.

As the evening unfolded, I became increasingly upset but held my turmoil inside. I could feel it building in the clench of my jaw, lava inside a volcano.

When everyone retired to their rooms, I assaulted Jill with words I wish I could erase. I'd sat there all evening, witnessing the other couples express their love through those nonverbal cues that two people give each other that say, "I love you. I'm having a great time in your company and I can't wait to lie next to you in bed later." A hand underneath the table that settles between a partner's legs, a suggestive glance, an unexpected kiss. It came crashing down on me that what those gestures meant was gone from my life. Our intimate lives had been struck from the face of this earth, while everyone else continued to enjoy theirs. And I had to stand by and watch.

Losing the ability to make love to my wife hurt as much as all the gut-wrenching spasms and burning torture I had to endure. I wrote to my psychiatrist, *I know time heals, but I don't think time will ever heal this one.*

I can see now that a part of the emotional pain I was suffering also centered on my loss of independence. I was used to being the one who determined my destiny, a quality I developed back when I was a skinny kid hell-bent on being a decisive figure in whatever sport I was playing.

In those first years after my accident, I was torn between the absolute necessity of dependence—on the various medications I had to take and the catheters, for example—and my drive to do things on my own, in my own way. My insistence when I probably should have acquiesced infuriated Jill more times than I can count.

I remember more than once needing to get a particular injection or have a minor procedure at a doctor's office and driving myself to the appointment. The nurses hadn't said that I *needed* to have someone else drive me and besides, I told myself, Jill was busy. No need to worry or disturb her, I'd tell her about how it went afterwards.

When I got home and shared where I'd been she'd shout, "Damn it, Bill, why didn't you ask for help!" She was usually right that what I'd done was stupid, that I should have asked for assistance. But I didn't know how to manage what I perceived as dependence.

Plagued by the anguish of the pain and all that I'd lost, and desperate to find relief, I submitted my tests and files to the neurology and pain management doctors at the renowned University of California San Francisco Medical Center in hopes that they would have a strategy for my situation.

In addition to reviewing my clinical file, they set up a visit with a psychologist. After a few initial questions she asked me, "So, Bill, what are you looking forward to?"

"Nothing."

"What makes you happy?"

"Nothing," I repeated.

"Is there anything that is remotely positive in your life that we can talk about?"

"No."

She glanced down at the papers on her desk. "I think we're done here."

And that's exactly how I was feeling too. Done.

The diagnosis from the medical team came back: *Definite evidence of arachnoiditis on the lumbar spine. Not surgically correctable.* Arachnoiditis is a particularly painful nerve condition that can be very frustrating because it's progressive and extremely difficult to treat.

I wrote to the doctor of reference: *My current situation is not acceptable to me long-term. I'm willing to take risks for improvement. Is there some procedure that could remove my pain in exchange for me being in a wheelchair?*

Boom. There it was. The pain had ground me to a pulp, to the point that I was willing to sacrifice my ability to walk, a part of me that I'd always considered indivisible from the rest of my being, as essential for my survival as blood and a beating heart. My worst nightmare, and yet it took on the appearance of a warm light shining through the window of a rustic cabin, and I was the lost hunter wandering in the wilderness. What I had fought so hard to avoid was now something I yearned for.

Grappling with the dilemma of dependence versus independence and dying versus living became a constant. Those days, months and years have become a patchwork of emotions, individual squares of color and shape that come into focus, triggered by memory.

My friend Annie and I were the same age and she too had been a serious high school and college athlete. In the prime of her life she discovered she had multiple sclerosis, unfortunately not the relapsing-remitting type but a form that attacked her aggressively. After her diagnosis, about the same time as I had my accident, she sold her house in the Bay Area and moved to a small town in rural northern California.

Each time I went up to visit her, the progression of her disease stared out at me, like an unwanted person in the room. I watched her progress through getting about on crutches, to a walker and finally a wheelchair; she and I understood each other in a way that only two people who feel doomed can.

Hey, Braveheart, she wrote to me in late 2010. *How are you doing?*

Our correspondence was often brutally honest. Serious illness or trauma has a way of destroying a person's modesty. *Not good,* I wrote, *but not terrible. I still can't feel my heels, back of my upper legs, entire buttocks, between my legs and genitalia. I have to stick a tube in my dick six times a day and a gloved finger up my ass once or twice a day and I always feel like I've got something up my butt. Lately it hasn't been overly large or overly hot, though. I'm in a constant medication haze. But recently I've been going to the gym and breaking a sweat on the stationary bike or the elliptical. I'm doing some upper body strengthening too. How about you, hot stuff?*

Things aren't good, Annie wrote back. She was becoming increasingly depressed and frustrated at how dependent she was on others just to deal with the daily activities of life. She had my total compassion. We were both proud and fiercely determined to be able to take care of ourselves and our needs. We'd spoken often about suicide and under what circumstances it might be warranted.

As the weeks marched on, her messages became increasingly bleak. She couldn't get in and out of bed or on and off the toilet without assistance and had moved, with her partner, into a small guest cottage on her parents' property next to the Pacific Ocean.

Then one day, instead of her usual weekly email I got a phone call. "Bill, if you want to see me again, you need to come now."

The next morning, Jill and I packed a light picnic lunch and made the four-hour drive up the California coastline. We arrived around noon, and Annie waved to us as we came up the dirt road.

After we all had lunch together out on the redwood deck, Annie's partner and I walked, just the two of us, toward the beach. With tears in his eyes and a quiver in his voice, he confirmed what I'd already understood. She was ready.

Her decision was devastating for me, too close to the reality we shared. Annie was fifty-seven years old and had a razor-sharp mind, but—and it's a big but—she could no longer look after herself. I totally understood. I too needed the help of my wife and sons but, fortunately for me, not nearly in the way she needed her partner and family.

Before Jill and I left, I hopped onto her bed and wrapped my arms around her. Jill took a few pictures. We cried together.

When I walked out of her home, I couldn't bring myself to turn around, to wave one last time. She died two days later. Ultimately, Annie had been unable to overcome what being dependent on others implied. For her, it was worse than dying.

Sad that my friend was gone but praying she was in a better place, I reassessed my own situation and latched onto one of the few things I had left—hope.

SIX

A LITTLE MEANS A LOT

When you feel like your life has been torn to shreds, sometimes what may seem tiny or insignificant to others can mean so much to you.

In the first five weeks after my accident everything was upended. I was in a hospital where sounds, smells and medical procedures swallowed me whole and I was stripped of the freedom to make choices. Since my immediate focus was on dealing with the shock of my situation and the desperate hope that I would somehow be able to walk again, I barely gave thought to the fact that my daily routine was far removed from my "normal" life. When you're loaded with pain medications and the other necessary drugs that keep you improving rather than losing ground, and you've got all sorts of tubes coming out of you, the loss of a full night spent in peaceful sleep can seem like a minor inconvenience.

But when I got back home—*our* home where everything was not only familiar but also reminded me of how massively things had changed—I yearned to curl up in our bed, pull the covers over my head and sleep until my body healed itself. But that was not to be. Instead, several days earlier, a hospital bed had been delivered and set up in our ground floor family room. And that's where I slept for almost a year.

Sleeping in your own bed in your favorite position is one of life's simple pleasures. While few people can actually put into words what it is about the smell of the sheets, the exact sag or firmness of the mattress or what it is about the composition of the pillow that offers them bliss, everyone recognizes it when they've got it, and when they don't.

I'm a sleep-on-my-side-in-a-fetal-position kind of guy. It's how I've always slept. However, due to my injuries I had to sleep flat on my back, on a hard mattress with an impermeable plastic cover like the one I remember we put on the boys' beds when they were learning to sleep without a diaper. Even the side bars on the hospital bed reminded me of a crib—I'd been exiled back to babyhood. And I had to sleep in the bed alone, without the warmth and comfort of my wife of thirty years. I felt as if I'd been banished as penance for some sin.

As the weeks passed and I began reacquiring independence and the ability to go about my new life, more and more I loathed having to sleep on my back in that damn hospital bed. And one day I decided I'd had enough.

I went to the bottom of the stairs and set one foot at a time squarely on each step as I had become accustomed to doing. Slowly, deliberately I climbed to the second floor. With my still uncertain gait, I made my way down the hall to the last door on the left. I entered the room and gazed at the object of my desire: our king-sized bed, where I'd awakened on that morning before driving to Mount Rose.

I approached the foot of the bed, ran my hand over the quilted bedspread then pulled back the covers and sat down on the sheet. I inhaled. Then, cautiously, I eased myself onto my side, let my head relax onto the pillow, and bent my legs to a comfortable angle. The bedding wrapped around me and I felt like I was lying on a cloud in heaven. I was engulfed in a reassuring security blanket—I was still me. At least this was one thing that hadn't been taken away, I told myself before I drifted off to sleep. My still broken body didn't find it totally comfortable yet, but it was definitely an improvement.

Eventually, I shifted fully from the hospital bed downstairs to our regular bed upstairs. However, it quickly became clear to Jill and I that, given my new medication-induced sleep patterns, it would be better if we slept in separate rooms. Not an ideal arrangement, but it was added to the growing list of changes I had to endure. Good, quality sleep is a priority and can make the difference between coping and having a meltdown.

There is one story related to this that still makes me laugh.

I've always slept best when my bedroom door is closed, and in my new set-up it was no different. Whenever Jill or one of the boys wanted to talk with me or check if I needed something, they would knock on the door before entering, as common courtesy would require.

One evening I was lying in bed but hadn't yet fallen asleep. I'd had a tough day and was in that in-between place that divides wakefulness from slumber. I heard what sounded like a knock on the door. "Come in," I said. There was no response so I drifted back into the semi-conscious state I'd been in before.

Once again, there was a knock but this time it was louder. "COME IN!" I shouted with irritation. Still no one.

What the hell was going on? I got up and interrogated my family. "Who's been upstairs knocking on my door, playing a bad joke on me?" They all denied involvement.

And then it hit me, right as a big, loud fart escaped from my body. Because of my spinal cord injury, I can't sense the passage of air through my digestive tract or feel when I'm about to pass gas. In bed, I'd farted and it sounded like a knock on the door.

We all had a good laugh, but the fact was that my new physical self was that unknown person on the other side of the door. Fifty-plus years of familiarity with its workings and habits had been cancelled and what remained was a stranger. I didn't only need to heal, I needed to get to know myself all over again.

One day, in the second spring after my accident, I looked in my closet. In all those months, it hadn't ever occurred to me to poke my head inside. Why would I? My wardrobe had become monotonous but functional: a pair of underwear with an incontinence pad, light sweatpants, a loose-fitting t-shirt, and footwear akin to high-top slippers that I could reach down and pull on by myself.

I stared at the button-down shirts, slacks, jackets, and stiff, black dress shoes I used to wear every work day. Maybe I'd be able to wear them someday, but for the time being, my usual outfit was fine. My days were occupied with going to the gym, popping briefly into my office, resting or taking a walk around the block with my dog.

The first time I tried putting my old clothes on I discovered that the pants no longer fit. I hadn't had to try on a pair of pants before buying them for years—I'd worn a 32×32 for decades—but now even a 34-inch waist was snug though a 36 was baggy. Proof, once again, that I wasn't the same guy. I was in a state of in-between too. Footwear was also a problem. My feet couldn't bear wearing shoes with a hard heel and rigid sole—they were enough to send me to bed in misery for a full day.

Formal occasions—whether professional or social—presented a dilemma. Poorly-fitting pants and tennis shoes could hardly be considered appropriate attire. Unable to find a satisfactory solution, we avoided formal socializing for a long time until I finally found a pair of dressier rubber-soled shoes and a good tailor.

All told, I spent many, many hours in bed. It was my sanctuary. On the really bad days I would be back under the covers before noon; even now, if I'm at home, I often spend several hours resting after lunch. It's a commonly accepted medical fact that a body needs sleep in order to heal.

When I'd go upstairs to lie down, Chipper would mosey along behind me. I'd shut the bedroom door then hear his body collapse onto the floor in the hall with a big exhale and thud as his chest hit the carpet. While I rested, he kept his nose and one ear pressed up against the crack under the door, ready if I needed him.

The length of time I napped was pretty consistent—about ninety minutes—and when I got up, Chip would get to his feet and follow me down to the kitchen where I'd give him a treat. He came to expect it each and every time.

However, when I was really hurting I'd spend two hours or more in bed, which meant a delay in getting his treat. I swear, I think Chip wore a watch. If I went past the ninety-minute mark, he'd whine as soon as I made the slightest sound that indicated I was waking up—a rustling of the sheets, a sigh. Then he'd get louder and louder the longer I delayed. If I started to chuckle behind the closed door, he'd reply with a full stream of barks.

Chipper was my companion for innumerable hours at home. He never let me out of his sight—he seemed to sense there was something wrong. He was as devoted to me as any member of my family and was actually a critical part of my recovery since every day he offered his canine version of distraction from reality. He was a constant reminder that a day would come—although I couldn't envision how far in the future—when life would be calm and steady.

With Chipper, 2016.

He and I would lay on the couch together or take a walk around the neighborhood. A healthy person would have been able to make the loop in fifteen minutes, but Chipper didn't seem to mind that it took me an hour. He never tried to make me go faster or do anything that I didn't initiate. So long as he was with me, his world was as it should be.

The non-judgmental comfort of a pet is another one of those little things that can mean so much. Chip's glossy black coat was soothing under my hand, his big brown eyes checked my every movement, his silky ears perked up whenever he heard my voice; he was my protector and companion in a way that another human couldn't be. That's not to say my family or friends were lacking in some way but with Chipper I never had to explain, apologize or worry that I was a burden.

Once I was feeling confident and able to walk on uneven ground, I'd throw on my hunting vest, take a shotgun and tell Chip to jump into my Durango. He was also an incredible game-bird dog. We liked to go to a place about an hour's drive from my house, what I called Disneyland for dogs. There was a river and streams, ponds and canals with lots of high grass. An ideal habitat for ring-necked pheasants. We had so much fun together, just the two of us. And bagging a few birds meant cooking and sharing the meal with friends and family—an added bonus.

There's no doubt in my mind about the value of pet therapy.

I took an important step toward returning to my active life in mid 2010. I was talking with the father of one of my son's teammates; the gentleman was in a wheelchair. "John," I said, "how do you deal with the depression of being confined to a wheelchair and all that goes along with it?"

Without hesitation, he said, "Hand bike." He explained that it's a bike powered by your arms rather than your legs and went on to tell me that it had rescued him from the depths of depression, as well as allowing him to create the upper body strength he needed to face life head on.

I ordered one for myself immediately.

A few days later I wrote in my journal: *Took my first hand bike ride today. Felt great to breathe hard again. My body feels a new strength and it's brought my lower body to life, creating a little more bounce in my step.*

That seemingly simple act of getting my lungs really working again in the fresh air and breaking a good sweat gave me an important boost. I'd faced uphill battles before and, in that moment, had confidence that if my body would allow me, success was attainable.

Later, when I was physically able to transition to a regular bike I sold the hand bike for almost nothing to another guy who'd suffered a spinal cord injury. I was glad to pass it on.

Because of all the medications, I had blood tests about every six months. In that same year I went in for the standard battery but, when the results came back, I was referred to my urologist, Dr. Bruno. My PSA level had shot up to almost 9, from 2.69 six months prior. A biopsy of my prostate was ordered.

"I don't know if I can handle any more bad news," I said as I entered Dr. Bruno's office when he had the results.

"Well, you have no choice. Your biopsy was malignant."

I collapsed into a chair, reeling from yet another blow. Hadn't I already taken my share of hits? When would I get a break? Cancer would be too much to handle on top of everything else.

Dr. Bruno outlined the situation and explained various treatment options, one of which was a prostate radioactive seed implantation. Many men prefer not to choose this type of treatment because it can lead to an inability to urinate and thus require catheterization.

Hell, I already had to catheterize myself multiple times every day! Choosing the seed implant was almost a no-brainer. This was my first chance to take lemons and turn them into lemonade, as the saying goes, and it was a fantastic sensation. A sort of small victory. And I'm happy to report that my PSA returned to an insignificant level.

Several years later, when my overall situation had stabilized and I was focusing on climbing the ladder toward my recovery, it became clear there were additional things

I could do to lighten my load. These weren't little things, I can assure you, but what I realized was that it's easy to lose sight of other fixable matters when all of your attention is directed toward your major setback.

For example, my knees were paying the price for high-level athletic participation as a teen and young adult: they were becoming seriously arthritic. Continued recovery from my spinal cord injury was going to be tough if I was also dealing with sore, swollen knees that limited my ability to exercise. I knew that from a recovery standpoint knee replacement surgery would be painful and demanding, but my vision had begun to shift from the immediate to the long-term. I carefully considered the risks and what the surgery would entail, then asked Warren for a referral since he didn't do full knee replacements.

I had one knee replaced, and then the other, about two years apart. It was a game-changer in the long run because I was able to reclaim the activity level that is so dear to me. Sure, needing to rehabilitate each knee after surgery added to my discomfort and complex workout routine, but I was already committed to strengthening my body. It wasn't particularly difficult to integrate specific exercises for my lower limbs and it was definitely worth it. Now, I've got two new, healthy and pain-free knees.

Other parts of my body were aging, as is normal for a man in his mid- to late-fifties. Another nuisance I decided to tackle was my worsening eyesight. One pair of glasses for reading, sunglasses with another prescription; reaching for the reading glasses at the office but discovering I'd left them at home. It was adding stress to my day-to-day, which was already difficult enough.

So, I took the leap and had lens implants inserted into both my eyes. Also in this case the procedures had to be programmed with a certain period of time in between and, for months, putting drops in my eyes was added to my daily routine. But living without glasses has improved the quality of my life tremendously, and when my hearing began to decline I had no doubt about turning to hearing aids.

Once you've begun to catch your breath after your trauma, don't lose sight of other things you can improve to offset the inconvenience of your primary injury. I don't want to give the impression here that running to a trusted surgeon is the answer to everything. No matter what challenge you're facing, always exhaust all other possibilities first before considering surgery. And if you still can't alleviate the problem, examine your various options and do what you can to fix the fixable.

This also applies in terms of medication: a little can mean a lot. At the end of the day, I was often exhausted and this impacted my pain, making it worse. Everyone knows that falling asleep while in the throes of pain is nearly impossible. So I started taking Lunesta before going to bed. With this approach I get six straight hours of REM sleep every night, which provides me with the restorative, uninterrupted rest my body needs so I can consistently work toward improved health.

Another simple pleasure I was able to enjoy was watching my youngest son Joe play baseball. Even when my pain level was high I would park on a hillside above the baseball field and, lying on a mattress in the back of my SUV, watch him through the window. Eventually, I graduated from the mattress in the car to using my walker to enter the stadium.

Toward the end of the 2011 baseball season Joe's team was playing at College of San Mateo and I planned to sit in the bleachers and support him, as my father had done for me. It was a beautiful, mild day, the type of spring afternoon in Northern California that makes sitting outside soaking up the sun's warm rays feel like paradise. It was that day when my most significant a-little-means-a-lot moment occurred.

As I was walking from my car to the baseball diamond, something in my stride felt different, although I couldn't put my finger exactly on what had changed. Later that day I wrote to Dr. Date: *I will forever be grateful to you for helping me persevere through this horrible injury. Without your encouragement I truly don't know if I would have made it. Today has been a great day. It seems like my whole body is trying to come back to life."* I had figured out what was different: I was experiencing feeling in the tips of my toes and the balls of my feet. I was so hopeful and at the same time afraid that maybe it wasn't true.

I often joked with friends, but one of those jokes that is steeped in truth: "You know, I don't have any feeling in the bottom of my feet or in my penis." Male listeners would generally have an expression of compassionate horror, considering what my words truly meant. "I have to tell you," I'd continue, "if I found a magic lamp with a genie who offered me sensation in one or the other I would have had no trouble choosing… the former." After a brief chuckle, the usual reaction was a silent nod as my words sunk in. I wasn't joking, I was dead serious.

The slight improvement I perceived on that spring day signaled that the marvel of nerve regeneration had begun. It felt like a miracle. A little meant so much.

SEVEN

MAKING ADJUSTMENTS

Everyone has heard stories about how blind people's intact senses compensate for their loss of sight. For example, the acuteness of their hearing is amplified and their ability to perceive their position in space becomes almost superhuman. People are amazingly adaptable when they need to be.

While playing college football as a freshman, I faced the option of making a major adjustment or giving up on what I'd been working toward for most of my young life. During a game against Boise State University I completely tore the anterior cruciate ligament in my knee. It was 1976, before present-day medical technology. My injury was irreparable and considered career-ending.

This wasn't part of the plan, I'd been awarded a scholarship to play ball. How could it have happened? I felt as if a huge storm cloud was hanging over my head, dumping rain and hurling lightning bolts.

There was, however, a faint ray of hope.

The orthopedic surgeon said there was a new kind of brace that some of the NFL players were wearing that kept an unstable knee from dislocating. With a combination of custom-fit metal and super strong flexible bands, the brace held the knee in position while allowing a good range of motion. It was big and unruly but, after strengthening my leg to the best of my ability, it allowed me to go back to playing ball. But not football.

It wasn't uncommon in the late '70s for university coaches to coach more than one sport, and the offensive line coach for the football team was also the head coach for baseball. He knew about my baseball accomplishments in high school and I asked if he'd give me a chance. He granted me a tryout—no guarantees, just an opportunity. I strapped on my brace and gave it my all. I made the team, and went on to play three, full 65-game seasons, starting at first base every single game.

The initial setback of the injury was tough but I overcame it. Baseball is inherently a game of adversity: even the best hitters fail two times out of three. It was this combination—of adjusting to the cumbersome brace and succeeding in high-level competition in a particularly challenging sport—that gave me the self-confidence to believe that I could overachieve when necessary. These are the roots of the mental toughness that I've come to rely on. In addition, pivoting toward another sport when my football career ended was an early step in the art of making adjustments.

Three decades later, there I was again, faced with a much bigger setback. As I attempted to cope with my new body, unexpected adaptations began to appear—abilities and adjustments, some seemingly out of the blue through no effort of my own, others as the result of the "try, try and try again" method.

For instance, one spring evening Jill and I were at home. As the sun lowered on the horizon it tinged the vineyard slope in our backyard with golden California light, marking the shift from the day's appointments, tasks and activities to a relaxing evening together. Sitting down for a cocktail before starting on dinner prep is one way we've always enjoyed unwinding at the end of the day. It's a nice segue into cooking.

That evening, I took two nice fat, rounded tumblers from the cupboard. I squeezed some lime juice into each one, filled them to the brim with ice, then added a shot of gin and topped them off with tonic water. I'd actually filled one of the glasses to overflowing and some of the liquid spilled over the side. Jill took her glass from the counter and I picked up the one that was overly full with my right hand and began to walk into the other room to sit down.

After a few steps, the tumbler began to slide from my hand. The liquid that had sloshed over the side of the glass was interfering with my grip and before I could get my left hand under it, it was gone. I could actually see the tumbler suspended in front of me. The cubes of ice, the transparent crystal, the sweaty outside of the glass. In a split second I reached down well below waist height and caught the glass as gravity pulled it toward the tile floor. Not a single drop was lost. It was the sort of catch any professional wide receiver would be proud to have captured on video.

Jill and I stared at each other with amazement, feeling we'd just witnessed a near miracle. How had I timed the catch so perfectly? How was it possible that nothing spilled from the overly full glass?

Before my spinal cord injury that cocktail glass would have ended up shattered on the floor, a million shards of crystal in a sea of ice cubes, gin and tonic. My manual dexterity after the accident has surprised me untold other times.

I chuckle with astonishment whenever I catch a slippery bar of soap midair while showering or grab onto the sink or a handle just in time to avoid disaster in the bathroom. For a person like me, bathing can be petrifying—all those smooth tiles, water, soap residue and hard surfaces—and trying to pick up a slippery bar of soap while standing in a shower stall poses a significant challenge, especially due to the lack of feeling in my feet. I can't count the number of times a sort of sixth sense in my hands has kicked in at the very last second.

These examples of heightened dexterity can't be mere coincidence. A nurtured body does, over time, find ways to compensate for the damaged parts.

In medical literature there's discussion surrounding recovery versus compensation after a neurological trauma. When is it a question of actually recovering function and at what point is it a reflection of compensation mechanisms? It's interesting to consider how our bodies adapt to a new situation but for a person like me with a spinal cord injury, the rediscovered function—no matter how or why it's there—is what really excites me. I'm glad the scientists are studying what happens after a neurological setback, but I'm even more grateful that my nervous system, damaged as it is, has found a way to help me out.

In addition to these unconscious reactions to a new physical status, adapting and finding unexpected strategies to cope with challenges is equally valuable.

I remember when, before my staph infection, the tendinitis in my elbow was so severe I couldn't participate in golf or tennis. Not being able to share those sports with friends, family or clients made me suffer as much as the physical pain did, maybe even more.

Then one day, I recalled something else about the wiffle ball my brothers and I used to hit in the backyard. My parents had given us an ultimatum: either play somewhere else or find a way to keep the ball out of the neighbor's yard. The neighbor had tired of having us drop down repeatedly onto his flowerbed and, quite honestly, it was a pain to have to climb the fence to retrieve the balls. So we set down a rule that when we played wiffle in the backyard, we could only hit left-handed. If there were major league baseball players who switch-hit, why couldn't we learn to do it too?

Stimulated by this memory, it dawned on me that maybe I could re-claim my happiness and also give my tendinitis a chance to heal by golfing left-handed. By reversing the side of the ball I was standing on, the pressure of the swing would go from the inside of my right arm—where I had the tendinitis—to the inside of my left.

Anybody who's played golf knows how difficult the game is. It took me several months of intense practice but eventually, I improved my left-arm swing to the point that I could get back out on the links with the people I enjoyed playing with. It was pure exhilaration being back out there, participating in the social pleasures of the sport I loved. Unfortunately, with time the tendinitis struck my left arm too and I transitioned back to playing right-handed, but the fact remains that I'd found a way to rebound from a limitation.

Going from being a healthy 52-year-old man with a deeply satisfying sex life with his wife to having what seemed like zero possibility of making love to her again was, understandably, devastating.

When Jill and I returned to Hawaii in early 2011 for the first time after my injury, I remember lying in bed going over in my mind what this trip used to mean and comparing it to what we now had. I sobbed and sobbed in my sorrow. It wasn't the first time I profoundly felt the loss, but being there, in that paradise-on-earth with my beloved wife, unable to partake in the bounty that surrounded me intensified my feelings of having been cut off from giving or receiving pleasure.

And back home it was no different.

How many healthy men in their mid 50's can imagine their wife saying, "Honey, can you please come back into the bedroom? It's been so long and I really want you to get in bed with me." And then the husband saying, "Sweetheart, I'm so sorry. I just don't feel like I can." That, roughly, was the repeated dialogue at our house.

To my amazement, however, my wife never stopped trying, never stopped asking. I believe she didn't care what our intimacy consisted of, but what mattered was that there was something. A little can truly mean a lot.

Eventually, as my physical pain subsided just enough and my wife persevered, we started to put our heads together. There had to be some options.

We tried pills and even tried a drug that had to be kept in a cooler until I was ready to inject it into the side of my penis to bring on an erection. Nothing worked.

So, again, I went to Dr. Bruno.

"We can fix this," he said.

My eyes widened. "Really?"

All I needed, he said, was the Titan One-touch inflatable penile prosthesis. "Instead of having two testicles, you'll have three. Whenever you want to get an erection you reach down, grab the middle one and pump about ten times and, bingo! It can last as long as you want. Then when you're done, you push a small button, squeeze your penis and the fluid that makes the erection goes back into the reservoir, ready for its next call to duty."

"Really, doc, it's that simple?"

"The hardest part is getting the insurance company to approve the surgery."

In my case, once the insurance company looked at my records I was approved immediately.

Of course, much more went into our return to a satisfying sex life but the Titan One-touch certainly kick-started the process.

Apart from the mechanical support, I've discovered what I like to call a brain orgasm. It's happened over and over. I can only explain it as a wave of very pleasant sensations that wash over me—a reasonably intense orgasm—initiated by my brain being turned on, for lack of a better term. It's different from what I knew before, but different doesn't mean unacceptable or insufficient. I see it as my body's way of adjusting to compensate for my deficit.

My loss of bowel control was another area where I thought outside the box.

Constipation is a common side effect of opiates prescribed for pain relief but without Oxycontin and other medications my life would come to a grinding halt.

I spent a long time—and lost a lot of underwear—trying to find the right balance between opiates and laxatives. The former caused me to be completely blocked; the latter would clear the way but seemingly always at the most inappropriate moment and totally outside my control. It was the worst humiliation imaginable. The difficulties surrounding this one facet of my new life had the potential to turn me into a person unable to go out into society, a recluse. All I wanted to do was crawl into a hole.

At a certain point, chronic constipation seemed like a better option than uncontrollable diarrhea and so I stopped taking the laxative.

For about a month practically nothing came out of my body. I felt irritable and was afraid of what might eventually happen but I persisted and trusted that my body would find a way to adjust. And finally it did.

I asked my urologist what he thought of staying constipated and dealing with it digitally. Without hesitation, he said, "It's absolutely fine so long as you evacuate the cavity." So now my middle finger (thank God for the invention of latex gloves!) takes the place of proper bowel function and I'm in control of my bowels rather than the other way around.

In order to do this on my own, I have to stay strong and healthy. My leg muscles have to be strong enough so I can hover above the toilet seat, my arms need to stabilize me and guide my hand under my lower body, and finally my hands and fingers require the necessary strength and dexterity to evacuate the cavity. This important independence relies on my staying strong.

What I have discovered is that by nurturing my body I was allowing it to find its own balance. Did my body reacquire exactly what I'd lost? No. But together my body and I found a solution to an obstacle that seriously limited my quality of life.

A number of times doctors have said to me, "Mr. Wallace, I don't think you should expect this function (whatever it might be) is ever going to come back or be what it used to be." It's devastating to hear those words and the most natural thing to do is to retreat into the depression cave and think your life is finished. But changed doesn't mean over.

Once, talking about the changes in my body with Warren, he told me, "Billy, everyone eventually loses feeling and function as they age, everything is taken away with time. It's just that you've lost them all at once!" That gave us a good laugh but, in all seriousness, by thinking about what kind of adjustment you need or can make in order to replace what you've lost, you're rebounding. Like a missed shot on the basketball court. Okay, so the ball didn't go through the hoop the first time, but by catching the rebound you get another chance to make the shot.

Not all adjustments involve the big issues like sex and intestinal health. Sometimes minor, everyday hurdles can be overcome by a little creative problem-solving.

When I was borderline well enough to go to the gym, a friend of mine who's a doctor called me. "I know what you're going through and I'm coming to get you. We'll go to the gym for some water aerobics. I know it's hard for you to dress and undress but don't worry, I'll help you." I was grateful for his offer since I hadn't yet learned how to ask for help.

At the gym we changed into our swimsuits and made our way from the carpeted locker room through a tiled area with a row of sinks toward the pool. My friend had his hand under my elbow as support but suddenly I slipped. I ended up sprawled on the tiles.

Everyone was in a panic. Someone shouted, "Call 911!"

"No, wait! Don't call," I demanded. "Don't anybody touch me." I needed to think. For several moments I ran through possible options in my head.

"Rob," I said to my friend, "go get a towel and put it under my butt. Then drag me to the edge of the hot tub. I'll put my feet in and then I can pull myself up on the railing."

By resisting the panic of others and thinking calmly, I was able to find a relatively simple solution to my predicament.

Adaptability quotient (AQ) has become a buzzword in human resources and the business environment. It's defined as an ability to adapt and thrive in a rapidly evolving environment. I think it's also a massively important quality when a person faces the aftereffects of a life-altering event.

It's true that a spinal cord injury or severe tendinitis are very different from the challenges of the modern business world, but the need to make adjustments and come up with and try new approaches is the same. I've learned that when faced with an obstacle, the most efficient strategy is often to think of a novel way to get around it rather than just charging at it head on like I was used to doing before.

But that doesn't mean taking a shortcut or an easy way out.

One of the most important adjustments I made was making time, every single day—no matter how badly I was feeling, to stretch, strengthen, and move my body. I'm living proof that a strong work ethic combined with a proper, adhered to exercise regimen can produce surprising results.

It took more than a decade to get strong enough to play back-to-back days of eighteen holes of golf with my brother and to tie his score each day—in other words, to play as equals. My brother is a top-notch golfer, he's physically bigger than I am, younger than I am, and does not have a spinal cord injury.

Golfing in Hawaii, 2019.

"I've *never* seen you play so well, Bill," he told me, not long ago at the end of our second golf day. "And not just since your injury. I mean it, the best ever—amazing!"

Despite the steel rod and titanium cage in my back, the seriously impaired sensation in my feet, and perhaps even thanks to my knee replacements, I was competitive again. I'd gotten there through consistent hard work driven by commitment to being the best I can be with what I have.

EIGHT

ACCEPT AND EMBRACE

Taking that first hand bike ride, nearly eighteen months after my injury, was a psychological turning point for me. Even though I was still deep in the throes of depression and plagued with chronic pain, it's when I took a tiny step toward acceptance. Being out in the fresh air, working up a sweat and feeling my heart pound in my chest reminded me what I loved about physical activity and personal challenge. Recognizing that my injury hadn't completely denied me of those sensations marked a breakthrough.

I had no illusions. I knew I had a very, very long way to go, an even greater uphill battle than when I'd had the staph infection. Recognizing this fact helped me admit to myself that *I* was going to have to change in order to reach a positive outcome. While the need for dedication and conviction were the same as the other times I'd gone through the rehabilitation process, the reality was that no matter how hard I worked, my spinal column would forever be damaged. Whatever I achieved would be my new normal. I was never going to be the Bill Wallace I was before. Forever and never are big words to face.

A family and marriage therapist we saw relatively early in the healing process also helped me progress toward acceptance. I think many people tend to dismiss and overlook the valuable support these professionals can offer following a significant setback. I'm glad I didn't.

After I told her what had happened, she said, "Well, in order for you to move on in a positive way you need to start accepting the fact that you're lucky enough to have two lives on this planet."

Lucky enough? I certainly didn't see it that way at the time.

She went on. "Your life as you knew it effectively ended on December 30, 2008. Rather than dying, you were reborn on January 1, 2009. That past life is never coming back. So, you can either mourn your death in self-pity or embrace the opportunity to get a two-for-one deal in the game of life."

What she said actually made some sense and did help me to mourn and grieve the end of my first life in a somewhat positive way. However, it took time.

Just as physical recovery comes as a slow drip, so does acceptance. I didn't just one day say, "Hey, this is all okay and I'm just happy to be alive." Hell no. I hated feeling vulnerable. I hated being unable to participate in the physical activities I adored. I hated feeling that every moment of every day and night was consumed with battling pain and concentrating on my broken body. I hated not being able to make love to my wife.

Getting my pain down to a tolerable level was a crucial part of my recovery equation and it allowed me to finally consider facing a future. My doctors and I had struggled, from the beginning, to find the right combination of pain medications. It seemed that every day was an ordeal. Would I succeed in staying on the right side of the suicide line that day? I didn't need to be wholly on the right side—one centimeter was enough—but the line was as clear to me as fresh lines painted on a tennis court. When the ball hits the asphalt, it's either in or out.

In November 2012 I took one final shot at trying to find a long-term solution for my pain. By that point, I was worn down with no grip, like an old pair of sneakers full of holes and a consumed rubber sole, ready to be tossed aside.

I went to a pain specialist who outlined various types of spinal cord stimulators and internal pumps that might be applicable in my situation. When I read his notes from our appointment, something shifted inside me.

He wrote: *Patient is taking 40 mg of Oxycontin every 12 hours. I reassured him he was well within national pain care standards but is just not getting enough relief despite being far more functional than I would anticipate. I'm quite impressed by his functional status as well as his ability to return to work and preserve his family and marriage despite this relatively devastating injury.*

I'm not sure what struck me in his notes, but in my gut I knew that another attempt at some kind of high-tech device to scramble the pain signals to my brain was not going to work. If something was going to change, it was going to have to come from me, from how my body reacted, from my way of dealing with the pain.

We made further adjustments to my meds that improved my situation—tweaking the dosage, shifting from fast-acting to time-release formulations, and administration intervals—and eventually my pain level evened out to something I could bear. One of the drugs my doctor prescribed was Nortriptyline, an antidepressant that can help with neuropathic pain. Unfortunately, it gave me horrible nightmares, which compounded my situation even more. Luckily for me, we found a relatively simple solution:

I could take it in the morning rather than before bed. It was a reminder that it's important to be receptive to doing things differently, to open your eyes to alternatives because sometimes that's where solutions hide.

The harsh reality was that I would never be pain-free but the time had come to accept it and move on, to commit myself to dealing with it.

I've done a fair amount of public speaking (both before and after my accident) in front of audiences made up of people trying to succeed in the financial services arena. I always end my talk with a quote from the Scottish mountaineer William Hutchinson Murray, although it's often erroneously attributed to the philosopher Goethe. Murray's words reflect upon the gravity of a very important word: commitment.

Until one is committed, there is hesitancy, the chance to draw back, always ineffectiveness. Concerning all acts of initiative (and creation), there is one elementary truth, the ignorance of which kills countless ideas and splendid plans: that the moment one definitely commits oneself, then all kinds of doors open that otherwise would not have.

This was the real change. I had exhausted all possible pain treatments and the only thing left was to accept the facts and commit, truly commit, to coping. To doing the best I could with what I had. From that point on, among my notes and the emails I wrote to doctors and friends, there's not a single mention of suicide.

Was there an ah-ha moment? A realization of victory like when the final buzzer sounds and, still breathing hard and drenched in sweat, you discover you've won the hard-fought game? No, I can't say there was, even though it would make great copy for this book. I simply shifted into wanting to live more than I wanted not to. After almost seven years, there had been enough drips into the bucket—I finally saw it as half-full, not half-empty. As I worked toward maximum improvement, my spinal cord injury seemed less overwhelming. As my strength, balance, and stamina improved, my pain, bowel, bladder and sexual dysfunction assumed a less commanding role in my outlook on life.

The only time I went to a physical therapist during my recovery was at the rehab center in Reno. I also asked my sister, who's a physical therapist, for advice but otherwise I guided my own rehabilitation. I'm not suggesting that other people follow my example, but I figured I knew my body, its unique situation, and prior history of surgeries better than anyone. Also, I was tired of appointments, and fighting traffic and the clock in order to be on time. I wanted to be the one in the director's chair.

My personal trainer, Michaela, and my massage therapist, Ben, supported me as my body slowly reawakened. We worked together toward a common goal: not to bring back the previous Bill Wallace (we knew and accepted that it wasn't possible) but to find out how far the new Bill Wallace could go. Just how brave was the heart that beat in this chest of mine?

I embraced every therapy session with the aim of making it the best I could do on that particular day. Michaela vowed not to feel sorry for me or play cheerleader but rather to push me (and, indeed, every workout I had with her was a ball buster!), and Ben gave me two hours of his best prodding and kneading every week.

Of all the areas of my body that were impacted by sensory loss, the soles of my feet have shown the greatest improvement. Ben would typically spend thirty minutes of our two-hour session working just on my feet. It took about three years to go from having almost no sensation in either foot to gaining about 25% of the sensation that an unimpaired person feels. It might not sound like much but the concept of a little means a lot really applies here.

I struggle to find the words to describe how life-changing it was for me to recover feeling in that part of my body.

Before, I was constantly fighting for balance and this unsteadiness had a way of impacting my general outlook on life. I didn't like myself and I'm sure others didn't like being around me. But regaining some sensation opened a doorway to a reconnection with the world around me, giving me grounding that otherwise might have remained elusive forever.

One thing that has surprised me is that I can still participate in activities that require balance and coordination.

Recently, Jill and I met a couple who are about our same age. They enjoy an active lifestyle, as do we, and suggested we play doubles tennis together. As happens frequently, we chatted and started getting to know each other as we played. The only detail about my health that came out was that I'd had both knees replaced.

At the end of three sets, the husband looked at me and said, "You really move well for a guy with two knee replacements."

"Well, let me tell you a story," I replied. I went on to tell him about my accident and having only 25% feeling in my feet. He was amazed and swore he would never have believed it was possible. And that's the way I feel too. I feel so God-damn lucky.

While I was working on this book, reflecting on my experiences and how my life has changed, a thought landed and resonated like a hole-in-one.

For my first fifty-one years, my masculine traits overpowered all aspects of my being. I spent my time focused on my physical abilities, with my eye on specific goals which were sports or money related or directed toward protecting my family. I thrived on competition with others and myself, and held onto the crazy idea that I was invincible. When I wasn't on a playing field, I plowed through life as if I had a football tucked under my arm, intent on reaching the goal line. It wasn't an image I was trying to project, it was me—that was my essence.

After my accident, a large part of my psychological suffering came from the fact that all of that was whisked away on a single winter's afternoon. In addition to being tormented by the chronic, debilitating pain, I agonized over the loss of myself.

What I had been was no longer, and I couldn't even begin to fathom what I might become. Half of my body refused to respond to my brain's commands, I was dependent on the assistance of others, and my inability to impose my will left me so frustrated I wanted to scream. The body I had counted on for my entire life had betrayed me.

Who was that stranger on the other side of the door, the unknown person who now inhabited my physical form?

If someone were to ask Jill or my boys about the early months, they'd say that I told nearly everyone I came in contact with about my accident. I'm sure they got tired of hearing about it. But the fact is, I talked about *it* not about how I was coping with the effects.

If Jill had been the one to suffer the accident instead of me, she probably would have surrounded herself with female family members and friends to help her grieve and deal with the changes in her life, giving and accepting compassionate care in a way that many men are unfamiliar with.

When I first got hurt and was newly back home, people rallied around. My difficulties were visibly evident: I used a walker or crutches and even when I was walking on my own, my gait gave away my condition. I didn't have to ask for help because it was given spontaneously, lovingly. Strangers held doors open for me and were patient when I was slow crossing the street.

With time, my body grew stronger and by degrees I adapted to my new self but that progress didn't erase my need for support and assistance. In my first life I'd never had to ask for help in day-to-day living, I felt fully self-reliant;

in my second, recognizing my limitations and acquiescing to the help of others was forced on me.

Part of embracing my new reality involved burying my pride, although I'm still a stubborn son of a bitch who refuses to take the easy road. However, with a lot of practice (and I do mean a lot) I've learned to speak up when I truly can't do something for myself and appreciate the willingness of others to assist me rather than resent it. I've even gotten to the point now where I can say to a stranger, "Excuse me, I have a spinal cord injury. Would you mind helping me?" And I feel just fine about it!

Learning to ask others for help has realigned my sense of compassion and empathy. I know what it's like to feel vulnerable—physically and emotionally—and I can't help but be more in tune with individuals who are struggling. For example, I have profound empathy for people who are fighting with addiction because I know firsthand what it means to surrender to a drug's power as it banishes blinding pain in an instant. I know what it's like to depend on the drug to get through the day. Now that I can walk, I leave disabled parking to those who truly need it because I remember a time when *I* couldn't do without it. This heightened awareness and understanding has added a dimension to my life that I never imagined.

Even my incontinence issues have made me a better person. I've learned how to be humble and how to be more nurturing toward my own body. I resisted using incontinence pads for a long time, and the result was that I had accidents. A pad seemed like a woman's thing. But eventually I realized that by accepting my incontinence fully, instead of fighting it, I became free. With a pad I could enjoy outings and activities and not have to worry. I went from outraged to grateful.

My new life has also meant added responsibility. Most people have three or four things they have to do before going out in the morning: getting dressed, brushing teeth, and so on. I have at least ten. Accepting those needs and embracing them—for example appreciating the necessity to catheterize myself with care means avoiding UTIs, meticulously following the procedures to refill prescriptions can mean the difference between anxiety and tranquility— these are the things that divide surviving from thriving.

The matter of prescriptions has been particularly trying. I have to take three medications daily that are on California's controlled substances list: pregabalin (marketed under the brand name Lyrica) for neuropathic pain, a time-release formulation of oxycodone (sold as Oxycontin) to block certain pain receptors in the brain, and eszopiclone (brand name

Lunesta) for sleep. As such, these drugs can only be dispensed—no more than a one-month supply at a time—by a licensed pharmacy upon compliance with clearly defined procedures: verification of the recipient's identity, confirmation of approval from the state of California, approval from the recipient's insurance company, and approval from the federal government. And then of course, the pharmacy has to have the appropriate quantity of medication in stock. I have no choice but to accept this system; if it were not for these drugs, I would not be alive today. If used properly, as my doctors have assured me, I will not become addicted, however I am dependent which means that if I don't take them every day at the prescribed frequency and dosage, brutal withdrawal symptoms will ensue.

These medications have become a part of our life—and I say 'our' because Jill has been my unfailing partner in managing them—for approximately eleven years. I've always gone to the same pharmacy in our town to get the little brown bottles, with DO NOT REFILL UNTIL… on the label, containing the precise number of tiny pills; pain-management doctors are allowed to prescribe 90 days of medicine between face-to-face visits with individual one-month prescriptions made out to cover the intervening period. So, doing the math, we can say that I've had to get my doctor to make out the three prescriptions about forty times and go to the pharmacy to have them filled about 120 times. Unfortunately, there have been maybe twenty times when the whole procedure has gone flawlessly from start to finish and the pharmacist has handed me the medications without delay. All the other times were screw-ups: the insurance company changed their paperwork; the State adopted new procedures; another document was needed from the physician, and on and on.

The stress linked to dealing with medications can be staggering. Until very recently, I felt pushed to the brink every month. As the pharmacy is closely regulated regarding the quantity and timing of distribution, every month I ended up holding my breath and praying that I wouldn't be left high and dry. And imagine what it's been like when travel was part of the equation. My head filled with questions: What happens if I run out of medication while we're away? Would a pharmacy in perhaps another state be able to fill the prescription? What happens if they can't? What if our return home is delayed and I run out of meds before we get home? If we schedule a departure for the day after my prescription can be filled, what happens if there's a problem and I can't pick up my meds before we leave?

Moreover, these pills are about one-third the size of the nail on your pinky finger and there are a multitude of ways and situations that can cause you to lose a pill or two over the course of thirty days. If that happened, it was tough shit. "Oh, Mr. Wallace, you say you've lost several of the pills…?" the pharmacist would say with a raised eyebrow and a suspecting stare.

This aspect of my life has been one of the worst parts of my injury because there are elements to it that are beyond my control and that cannot be circumvented. The ceaseless ordeal is a beast that can emerge from its cave at any time, threatening my hard-won equilibrium. The sidelong glances, suspicious demeanor and interrogations at the pharmacy are humiliating.

Jill has suffered by my side every step of the way, filling those seven-day pill cases week after week, counting the pills and calculating windows of opportunity to get away for a few days or showing the doctor our airline tickets in hopes that he'll add a few extra days on to a single prescription. And when I'm stuck without medication, Jill's my rock.

Over a recent long Thanksgiving weekend, the umpteenth fiasco occurred with regard to my Oxycontin prescription. I went to the doctor's office, hoping to clear things up, but he was away. I had no more pills. It didn't take long for the initial withdrawal symptoms to begin: sweating, blurred vision, frequent blinking, stiffness in my joints.

From what I'd read, the worst of the withdrawal lasts seven to ten days. Maybe I could tough it out and give up taking the drug, I considered. I wouldn't be as comfortable on a daily basis after breaking through the barrier, but I would be willing to accept that if it meant freeing myself from this monkey on my back. I've gotten used to so many unpleasant things, this would just be one more. "I can do it," I said out loud, recalling how my physical fitness had helped carry me through my early recovery, although inside I was scared to death. If it doesn't kill me, I'll get through it.

After four days, I wrote to a friend, *Not feeling great but not terrible either. It's one hour at a time until I climb out of this hole. I will persevere.*

Finally on the eighth day, my withdrawal symptoms subsided. It had been a very long week, but not as bad as I had imagined it would be. One thing was certain: Oxycontin effectively reduced my pain and definitely improved my quality of life. More importantly, though, I proved to myself that if I was ever without it, I could survive. I could choose, if necessary, to wait it out if the bottle of pills tipped over and I lost two of them rather than be subjected to suspicion and disbelief. There was no need to panic. Fate had offered me an opportunity—in the form of an incorrectly written prescription—to understand that I *can* choose. It was as if the big, dark cloud that had been hanging over Jill and I threateningly dissipated and the sky now was only partly cloudy.

My life is much better because of this drug; I continue to take my regular, daily dose. I'm thankful that it exists and that the State recognizes my medical need, but now I understand that I'm no longer a slave to the bureaucracy, red tape and regulations.

What felt like the last barricade had finally been knocked down.

NINE

THE HAPPIEST PEOPLE DON'T HAVE EVERYTHING

(they just make the most of what they have)

Every year the insurance company I worked for hosted a holiday party to recognize people's accomplishments over the previous twelve months and provide an opportunity to talk about the future. Included in the annual program was an invited speaker who generally imparted some motivational message. In 2014 the company asked me to be that speaker.

After a fair amount of thought, I decided that since the party coincided with a time of year when people usually reflect on what they're grateful for and the gifts they have in life, I would touch on how fragile good health can be and how it's not something to take for granted.

The mood for the evening was warm and friendly among the 150 people in attendance, who were area employees with their spouses or partners. All of them were aware I'd faced a major trauma but as my office was detached from the primary regional office suite, most of them hadn't seen me since before the accident.

When I stepped up to the microphone, I began reminiscing about the 2008 holiday season, before everything changed. I shared how Jill and I had enjoyed a wonderful Christmas celebration in our home with family and friends and how, after the guests left, we commented on the evening upstairs in our master bedroom.

Sitting on the edge of the bed, I took off my shoes then padded barefoot toward the bathroom, noticing with each step how soft the carpet was. As I crossed the room I glanced at Jill and we exchanged some of that nonverbal communication between partners that conveys the promise of shared intimacy. In the bathroom I took off my clothes, emptied my bladder and then crawled into bed next to my beautiful wife, anticipating the physical and emotional gifts that people in love share with each other, and the prospect of a good night's sleep.

Little did I know that would be the last time in my life I would ever be able to experience those things. A few days later, in less than a minute, they were stripped away.

As I gave my speech, I let my mind travel to that evening and the sensations. Absorbed in the memory, I realized that I'd lost visual connection with my audience for a moment. Turning my focus back to the people in the room, I became aware of the tears in their eyes. Some had them rolling down their cheeks. A silver-haired gentleman I knew well took a handkerchief out of his pocket and wiped his eyes. I saw one of the support staff reach out and squeeze her husband's hand.

Hastily, I wrapped up my talk, wished everyone an enjoyable evening and stepped down from the podium. Maybe I'd gotten too personal. Maybe I should have stuck to a lighter topic. All I wanted in that moment was to be out of the spotlight. As quickly as my legs would carry me, I made my way to the bar outside the banquet hall where the reception would soon shift.

Standing behind the polished bar was a lone, young female bartender. When I got close enough to see her face, I saw that it too was streaked with tears. Unlike the guests at the party, she didn't know me nor had she ever heard anything about what I'd experienced, and yet something in my story had touched her.

That's when a seed was planted: maybe by sharing my story I could help other people. Maybe I was being given an opportunity to take what I'd gone through, what my family had endured, and turn it into something greater that could inspire others; a harrowing life-changing event could become something positive. I truly believe the genesis for this book began on that evening.

I've been forced, by writing this book, to step away from myself, my family and my everyday life in order to get perspective, to examine the significant and seemingly insignificant events and try to make sense of them all.

Like most everyone who faces an unexpected trauma, I too asked myself early on, *Why me? Why now? What caused this?* These questions don't undo what happened nor do they help you move toward your goal of recovery. They can be distractions. When you're truly focused on and committed to reclaiming as much of your prior condition as you can and are willing to accept what you can't change, details and interrogations that pull you away from your objective end up by the wayside. Flimsy remnants of a past experience.

I suppose I could have sued the ski resort, but honestly it never crossed my mind and I'm glad it didn't. It would have confined my field of vision to the accident and not allowed my recovery to take center stage. I realize I'm lucky because I had the option to choose, knowing that financially we had what we needed, but some people who suffer injuries commit the majority of their energy to the battle for justice and end up short in the fight to regain health. It's important to get your body geared for recovery and actively working toward it as soon as possible after a setback. Time and energy lost can rarely be recaptured.

Looking back on my fears and anxieties, I realize that a good number of them were, in the long run, unfounded. Of course, at the time, I had to go through the grieving process for my lost life and learn to make the necessary adjustments, but I'm much happier and content with my life now than I ever thought I could be. In fact, it blows me away when I think of how distraught I was about losing my life as I knew it, and conversely how at peace I am with it now.

It's true that Jill and I, as a couple, suffered incredible losses as a result of my injury but rebuilding our life and doing it together has given us an amazing opportunity to strengthen our relationship. We've discovered that the struggles and accomplishments—undertaken together as a team—can be unbelievable journeys in themselves. As the saying goes, it's not the destination but the journey that's important.

Part of what drove me to contemplate suicide was that I couldn't imagine my life ever having meaning again.

Now I'm so glad that I stuck it out. And Warren was right. Suicide does end the pain but it also ends everything else: the joy of having an incredible wife by my side, the love of our sons and witnessing their future, amazing friends. A person's family and friends never stop needing them. Since the accident, there have been at least three hundred times that my sons have come to me for advice. "Hey, Dad, I need your opinion…" I was so wrong to believe that the only thing they needed from their father was some good financial planning.

All three of my sons have been an amazing part of my recovery. While my body was no longer the one they were familiar with, the fact that my cognitive world was unchanged meant that I was still the same person. I think this helped them, and helped us maintain our strong relationship. Over the course of these years I've proudly observed how they coped with the shock and adjustments, each in their own way. But more than anything, I've watched them move into full adulthood with experiences and outlooks that can only make them better men. My accident has not only been transformative for me, but for them as well. We're all stronger because of my spinal cord injury.

Now I have two absolutely wonderful daughters-in-law too. Craig and Laurie-Anne were married in 2014, and

Bret and Addie in June 2016. Since Jill and I have only sons, they are my first experience with girls and I feel blessed to have these loving, compassionate and intelligent women as part of our family. My sons are lucky guys.

I remember a flight back from Hawaii one year. I was physically well enough to make the trip, but I wasn't completely in the clear from an emotional standpoint. In the seats in front of Jill and I were two grandparents with grandchildren on their laps. Jill made some comment about how maybe one day we could share Hawaii with grandkids. Rather than inspire me to persevere, the idea fell flat at my feet, like a basketball that's lost all its air. In my heart I hoped I would never become a grandfather—I didn't want grandchildren to know me and then have me be gone, I thought I was too broken and didn't see a long life ahead of me.

Fortunately, as with many things, time has a way of healing.

In the beginning of 2019, Craig and Laurie-Anne gave us the news that our first grandchild was due in August. Knowing our family was growing, that a new generation was on its way, filled me with gratitude and joy. To think I was willing to cut myself out of this picture prematurely.

I've been amazed at how, over the years, my love of family has grown exponentially. I loved my family before, but thanks to Jill's modeling of true dedication and loyalty day after day and without hesitation, my devotion has reached a new level. Even in my professional life, family is a pillar, an integral part of the equation.

When Joe finished college, he began working with me in the insurance business. His youth and unique perspective injected energy into what I'd built over a thirty-year period. It wasn't long, though, before he encouraged me to consider transforming what we did for our clients. He suggested opening our group to new opportunities so we could offer independent financial planning services. He also reminded me that it was important to transition the relationships I'd cultivated. Nowadays, when the phone rings in the office, eight times out of ten it's not for me, and that's the way it should be. If we are encouraging clients to plan for their future, we need to model what that looks like.

Craig has since brought his own expertise to the team, overseeing operations and compliance. Together our group focuses on preserving and putting to work the financial assets of families with their future generations in mind. Families take care of each other—it's one of the things we've learned from my recovery. And I like to believe that by asserting this core value, not only through thoughtful financial guidance for our clients but also through our family-centered approach that combines the strengths of several generations, we're helping others make the most of their families and whatever comes their way. I'm a firm believer in prepping yourself for the big games in life, and prepping in financial terms is no different.

Everyone always thinks that misfortune is going to knock on the other guy's door. For me, it didn't work out that way.

Jill used to refer to Chipper as my fourth son. He was a part of our family, unconditional love and affection on four legs.

On three occasions during the twelve years he was with us, he managed to find chocolate stashed away in what we thought was an out-of-dog-reach place. Each time we found empty wrappers littering the floor and him shaking like a leaf, proof of his illicit and dangerous indulgence. As anyone who has a dog knows, chocolate is toxic for canines. Three times we rushed him to the vet who promised to do his best to save Chipper but with no guarantees. To our relief, our beloved pet pulled through every time. And every time, as soon as we went home, we vowed to find a more secure place for any cocoa-based confection that might end up in our house on Rose Lane. Clearly, Chipper loved the taste of chocolate.

The other thing Chipper loved was lying outside my bedroom door, guarding me during my afternoon rest, and then getting his reward in the form of a dog treat for a job well done. Sadly, as the years passed, we noticed that his reactions became a little slower and his legs stiffer—unmistakable signs that he too was aging.

One afternoon, I started up the stairs and, instead of him following at my heels, he sat down heavily at the bottom of the staircase and stared at me. He wouldn't budge but barked and barked. Not the sort that alerts about danger or the bark of play, rather it was a yelp of distress. My poor buddy Chip could no longer climb the stairs. Like my friend, Annie, his body had deteriorated to the point that his pain blotted out the possibility for pleasure.

He had also started becoming seriously depressed whenever he heard us unzip suitcases—the anxiety and grief of a weakened soul, alone, dispirited, and afraid. Jill and I had several trips coming up and we knew our preparations and departure would be agony for him. I had firsthand knowledge of what it meant to suffer, and didn't want to make him go through the pain any longer.

The dreaded day eventually came when I knew it was time. Jill was out of town and the boys were all living elsewhere, so it was just Chipper and me.

I went to the gym in the morning and when I came out at about noon I stopped off at the frozen yogurt shop. I ordered an extra large swirl of vanilla and chocolate with a great big chocolate chip cookie on top, then drove straight home.

Chip was waiting for me as I pulled into the garage. I got out of the car and set the heaping bowl down next to his mat. Without a moment's hesitation, he gobbled the cookie and his big pink tongue lapped at the melting yogurt until there wasn't a single drop left. With tears in my eyes I told my friend to get in the car and we took the ten-minute drive to the vet's.

When we got there, they led him into a room and gave him a shot of a muscle relaxant. He slumped to the floor and I sat down next to him, my hand resting on his smooth black fur, feeling the up and down movement of his chest with each breath. "Are you ready?" asked the veterinarian, syringe in hand. I nodded, unable to verbalize.

Seconds after the injection, his chest stopped moving.

All the way home, I cried like a baby, just as I'm crying as I write these words. Chipper was the only pet we'd ever had, an irreplaceable part of our family. I miss him terribly but know that I did right by him.

While I was going through photos and notes to write this book, I decided to make a list of all the places I've visited and special experiences I've had over the last eleven years. It's a long list. I was surprised by all that a physically limited human can do.

I've discovered that with adequate planning, travel to almost any destination is possible for someone with disabilities. One of the themes from this book comes heavily into play when you're looking to expand your horizons after a major setback: making adjustments can lead to getting around obstacles rather than crashing into them head-on.

Jill and I have been fortunate enough to travel internationally, take active family vacations, and participate in professional events in luxurious settings. Each and every trip has presented unique challenges—from managing prescription drugs and catheters, organizing group activities that will satisfy both energetic 30-year-olds and an enthusiastic but disabled 60-year-old, to finding acceptable formal wear that meets my needs. But what's important is that we've been enriched by our shared experiences. Really, from a planning perspective, it's not much different from when we traveled with small children—we survived that experience and came away with some fabulous memories, so why shouldn't we travel now?

During a recent flight home from Reno I got a bird's eye view of the mountain where I had my accident. The sight of the steep, snow-covered ski runs caught in shadow felt like a punch in the stomach. What the hell was I even doing on that cliff face in the first place? I regret that, at the time, I didn't fully consider the consequences of pointing my skis down that slope. As I was looking out the window of the plane, I realized how far I had come since the accident and remembered all the truly amazing days I've had since then.

Like the day I succeeded in riding my bike up a 3800-foot free-standing mountain.

Mount Diablo is a well-known Bay Area landmark and one of the most impressive 360-degree views in the western United States awaits those who reach its summit. Before my accident, cycling up it was always a great way to check my aerobic conditioning. It's thirteen miles of steady incline, the final segment of which starts with a hairpin turn called the Devil's Elbow and a grade of about 15%. It's a bear of a climb.

Climbing Mount Diablo on my bike was tough in my prime, but after my accident it seemed unattainable. All the same, I held it in my mind as a challenge that would—if I overcame it—confirm that I'd reached full recovery.

I seriously trained to reach my goal, with one-set-to-exhaustion as my mantra and my dogged determination as strong as ever, and kept repeating to myself that it was only a matter of time until the exhilaration of the conquest would be mine.

As I approached the ten-year anniversary of my injury, my lower body strength and cardiac fitness had improved dramatically. My legs kept getting stronger and stronger and on the stationary bike I was doing some really hard climbing. Not wanting to fail, I kept training, tracking the tiny improvements as the months passed, confident that I would know when I was ready.

Then, one spring day, I called my son Bret. "Do you want to ride up Mount Diablo with me?" After his initial surprise, we made plans and on the following Saturday we loaded our bikes into my car.

We started off together and before long found our rhythm, pumping our legs as we travelled up through the scrubby, chaparral vegetation and exposed rock. After the halfway point, Bret rode on ahead with the idea of reaching the summit then coming back down to ride with me or help me in the final ascent. He took off and I kept pedaling at my pace, focusing on my breathing and the sensations in my thighs.

At about the two-thirds mark, Bret appeared and circled his bike so he was next to me. "You've gone far enough, Dad."

"No, Bret. I've been thinking about this for ten years," I insisted, between heavy breaths. We continued pedaling. "Go to the top and watch me do the last part. If I start to fail, help me up the rest of the way."

The final slope was so steep that I couldn't get off my bike, even if I'd wanted to. My whole body—head, shoulders, arms, and chest—was tense, working in tandem with my thighs to turn the pedals, my focus glued to the asphalt in front of me. Just like when I took my first unaided steps.

At about twenty yards from the summit Bret jogged down to where I was. "You can do it, Dad! Come on, you can do it!" he shouted at my side.

And I did. And just to be sure it wasn't a fluke, I did it again two months later.

Riding up Mount Diablo, 2018.

Interestingly, the idea of my getting back on skis hadn't even flickered in my mind in those years. Not even after I emerged from the suicidal thoughts. I gave away the various ski equipment I owned, convinced I would never use it again. Returning to the scene of the crime held no attraction for me.

But then, rather suddenly, I thought, "Why not try skiing again?" I started joking about it with friends and my sons, to try on the idea. If Jill was in earshot, she never laughed or smiled with us. Bringing up the topic had her hyperventilating in a matter of seconds.

"Billy," said Warren, one afternoon, "I'm going to take you up skiing and we're going to write the last chapter of your amazing recovery!"

Well, if Warren, with his professional experience thought I could do it… I let the idea's seeds take root.

In February 2018, I was boarding a plane in Hawaii. I had to get back to work, but Jill was staying on for a few more days. I heard my cell phone *bing* with an incoming text message.

How would you feel about going skiing Tuesday?

My son's message caught me by surprise. The tropical climate had kept any errant thoughts of snow and skis at a distance.

Well, I thought, it depends. Possible scenarios flashed through my mind. What if something went wrong again?

Was I willing to take a chance? How was the weather forecast? How about the snow conditions and visibility?

They just got a big dump, two feet of fresh powder. They're predicting a blue-bird day, not a cloud in the sky, light breezes.

If I were to go, I'd have to have reliable gear. After what I'd been through, I wasn't willing to risk faulty equipment.

There's a place in Truckee where I've gone before. The guy knows his stuff.

I considered what Jill would think. If I was ever going to do it, it would be easier to ask her for forgiveness than ask for her blessing. The only way this could happen would be with her out of town.

Mentally I assessed my physical condition. There was no doubt I had issues but I'd counterbalanced them with adequate training. My workouts would have been tough even for an able-bodied man of my age. I was sixty-one years old and my physical and mental shape was the best it could be with what I had. It's now or never, I thought.

Two days later, before the sun came up, Craig, Joey and I got in the car. My memory of that other time, all those years before, reappeared in my mind's eye but didn't scare me. Knowing that my sons would stay close and watch over me was immensely reassuring. Father-son devotion is a two-way street. We didn't talk much on the three-hour drive to the Alpine Meadows resort. They respected my state of mind, and I can guess that they were dealing with their own anxieties too.

Craig and Joe had decided to take me to Alpine because of the numerous intermediate runs it offers. My days of skiing the double black-diamond ones were over for good.

We stopped at the rental shop on the way and I discovered that skis had changed in the nine and a half years since I'd last hit the slopes. They'd become shorter and broader, with greater surface area, which was definitely a plus for me. On the other hand, when I tried on the boots I started to have second thoughts. My feet felt like they were encased in cement bricks. Heavy and clunky, the boots obliterated what little feeling I did have.

The reality of the sensation fully set in once we parked at the ski resort and had to walk the five hundred yards to buy tickets and get on the chairlift. What I'd perceived in the shop became multiplied by a hundred. The signals flowing to my brain were pure electricity, rapid-fire and ominous. But despite the quivering in my gut I yearned to test myself. I needed to feel the snow under my skis, to know if I could do this.

I sent Jill a selfie video several hours later as I was going up the mountain on the chairlift, telling her what a great day I was having. Given the three hour time difference, she was asleep when I sent it.

While Craig, Joe and I were having lunch, my phone started going crazy with incoming texts.

Bill, I'm very happy for you. Glad you got it out of your system but that will be both your first and last time skiing after the accident. Maybe, at the most, together we can teach our grandchildren to ski someday.

Skiing, 2018.

In the early hours of August 16th 2019, Laurie-Anne's water broke. I was alone in Hawaii working on the book when I got the news.

Hours passed and still no baby. Jill reminded me that twenty-four hours of labor is not uncommon for a first-time mother. When I crawled out of bed the next morning and discovered there'd been no change, my excitement about finding out if it was a boy or a girl faded into concern.

Finally, on the 17th, I saw Jill's number on my phone and picked up immediately. Her voice was trembling. "There's a problem." Apparently the baby had become distressed and they had rushed Laurie-Anne into surgery for an emergency cesarean section. Then they had difficulty getting the baby to breathe and had to force oxygen into its lungs. Knowing that a person's trajectory in life can change in an instant, I understood the outcome was uncertain. "It's a boy. Nine pounds, four ounces," said Jill. Craig and Laurie-Anne had decided to name him Cooper.

Well, I thought, however things work out we'll come together as a family and we'll love and raise that child just like we raised our three boys. I was concerned for the safety of my daughter-in-law and the baby, but felt no panic that our grandchild might not be perfect. Sometimes life throws shit at you when you least expect it and, if that happened in this case, I felt certain the strength of our family unit would carry us through, just as it had carried me through my darkest moments.

Within thirty minutes, Jill was on her way to the airport to fly to Portland to advocate for Laurie-Anne and Cooper, like she'd done for me when I was in the hospital.

The next morning she texted me that the crisis seemed to have passed and all indications were that Cooper was healthy. Silently, I thanked God for the quick reactions and snap judgment of a well-trained doctor at the hospital.

Proud grandparents, 2019. (*Photo by Daisy Coby*)

The joy of being a grandparent has exceeded anything I could have imagined and I look forward to being a part of Cooper's life as he grows and develops into the person he's meant to be. Nowadays, my plan is to be around for a long time.

Only a few days short of the eleven-year anniversary of my accident our family celebrated Christmas. Our home was full of love, the sounds of a happy baby, and the smells of holiday cooking. I couldn't help but think of two other Christmases past.

Perhaps the most obvious one—the last one that belonged to my old life—I recalled with fond appreciation, like the memory of a valued mentor who has since left this earth, leaving in his wake lessons learned.

Instead, memories of Christmas 2009 clenched so tightly at my heart that it hurt. That year we had a huge family gathering. Everyone came, including Jill's sister, husband and daughters from Switzerland, her brothers and their families, and my in-laws. It was the first holiday season after my injury and they'd come to show their support for me, for Jill, and our boys. There's a photo of everyone together. Everyone but me. I was upstairs behind my closed bedroom door, in too much pain and agony to come down for the photo or dinner. I'll never forget hearing the joy and laughter that was going on downstairs and weeping until I had no more tears to cry. I was so lucky to have all those people who loved me but felt miserable because I couldn't show them how much I appreciated their support or share in the celebration of life.

These days, a decade after that painful Christmas, my life is finally calm and steady. I'm so glad I didn't give up, but instead chose to allow the magic and wonder of life, buoyed by my hard work and commitment, to amaze me on a daily basis. Time and again, my body has surprised me and, no matter what adversity you might be facing, yours has the ability to surprise you too.

EPILOGUE

During the final stages of writing this book, the coronavirus pandemic exploded. Shock, fear, and a concern for the future unite us all in this shared, global trauma. The world we knew has changed due to an unexpected event beyond our control and I've discovered that the underlying feelings and anxieties are incredibly similar to my story of personal trauma. There's a clear-cut before and after.

Prior to December 30, 2008 it was impossible to imagine that my life would change so dramatically and profoundly. For months following my accident, I had no hope of ever enjoying life again. But somehow, I survived and rebuilt.

While writing this book, I realized that my first life prepared me for my second life. All along, unknowingly, I was acquiring the skills to face a life-altering event. I knew about diligence, determination and adapting, while appreciating what I had and accepting and embracing my new reality came with time. A particular sequence of actions is not what got me through my personal hardship, instead it was an approach to adversity—a complex weave of experiences not limited to my tumbling down a mountainside—that made recovery possible.

I'm coming up on the twelve-year anniversary. Our family continues to grow (Bret and Addie have announced they're expecting their first child at the end of 2020) and my body continues to surprise me with improvements in balance, strength, sensitivity, and endurance. I've achieved things I never, in my wildest dreams, thought would again be possible. Recovery is without a defined destination, what it offers are opportunities waiting to be discovered. We can't imagine now what awaits discovery as we navigate this new coronavirus world, just as I couldn't imagine as I leaned on crutches to walk across a room how my life and love would change for the better. By striving to improve whatever is within the realm of the possible, accepting what can't be changed and making the necessary adjustments to live with those limitations, a rewarding, meaningful life is accessible to anyone.

When an acquaintance first suggested that I tell my story through a book, I discarded the idea almost immediately. What did I have to offer? I was barely getting through each day. But as time passed and I had conversation upon conversation with people about my experiences—in particular doctors treating patients who were suffering—they kept urging me to share, unaware of the future that awaited us all. What story will we one day tell, together?

I hope that these pages may inspire, not only when there's physical adversity or an emotional setback, but also in this shared trauma and whatever we face together in its aftermath.

A NOTE FROM JILL

I have to confess that when I realized Bill was serious about writing a book to tell the story of his accident and recovery, I was unsure how I would react to reliving the experience. My survivor mode had always been based on the motto "One day at a time" and looking back was not something I really wanted to do. I feared that seeing the particulars of Bill's journey printed on a page would bring back the emotional rollercoaster and remind me of those dark days. That's not to say our lives are perfect now but I'm relieved the worst is behind us and want it to stay that way. My own version of recovery included learning to let go of the painful details.

I procrastinated for a long time before actually picking up the manuscript but, eventually, I read the whole thing in one sitting. Bill and I both knew my blessing was needed before it could be published; too many specifics about our personal lives were going to be exposed. I'm a very private person and there was legitimate doubt that I would accept having our intimate details included. Bill had worried that reading it would make me cry, but I didn't allow myself to feel pity or sorrow. For years now, they are not part of my life. Instead, getting his story down on paper offers a unique chance to help others face their challenges and I was certain Bill would be more at peace with his future knowing he was turning his accident into something positive.

My husband has poured his heart into this book. After more than forty-five years together, he's still the same: he's persistent and true to anything he tries to accomplish. That's what has gotten him past the countless hurdles on his way towards recovery. Living up to his standards is not easy, but I do my best.

For my part, I've never wavered in my role as a caregiver—he's my husband and we made vows that were not to be broken. As a married couple, the changes we had to endure seemed unending, but one fact always remained the same: he was the one in physical pain and there was no way I could feel sorry for myself. The truth is that, through it all, our love has grown to another level.

The gratitude we have for our family and friends stretches beyond words. I can never thank our sons, their beautiful wives, our immediate families and close friends enough for all the support and love they have shown us. The accident is and always will be a part of the man I love and I accept that fact unconditionally. I could not be prouder of him.

ACKNOWLEDGMENTS

"A friend is someone who understands your past, believes in your future, and accepts you just the way you are."

—*Unknown*

There are so many people who have contributed to my recovery, and thus to making this book possible. These few words of recognition are a meager substitute for my deepest gratitude.

My family has been at the center of it all. I honestly would not be here if it weren't for their love, strength and support. I thank my parents, Mardelle and Bill, whom I miss terribly, for having instilled in me a solid work ethic and modeled through their lives the strong moral values I strive to emulate; Jill, who has never left my side; my sons Craig, Bret, and Joe, and daughters-in-law Laurie-Anne and Addie who, with their youth, urge me to be youthful and allow me to be part of their lives, their spirit is an inspiration; my brother Mike and his wife Vicky, and my sister Susan and her husband Bill who have stood by me in times of both darkness and light; and my coach and father-in-law Jerry Scattini and my wonderful mother-in-law Diane for loving me like a son. I'm also profoundly grateful for the rest of our extended family and appreciate their willingness to rally around us when times have been tough and share in celebration when there've been victories.

I have been blessed with two special friends who are as close to me as brothers and I eternally thank them for all they've done for me. Warren King—my childhood buddy and later trusted surgeon—first helped me grow into manhood and then, through his skills and knowledgeable advice, guided me toward the quality of life I enjoy today. I would also be at a loss without my friend Mike Piotrowicz. He looked after my sons like a father when they were studying far from home and his expert mentorship in my professional life has impacted my family and clients in more ways than I can count. Both of these men have all my esteem, respect and gratitude.

There are also two women who I could not have done without, especially during my recovery, and whose continued support and dedication I appreciate immensely. Julie Ortega has been my assistant for thirty-five years and Dawn Freccero has been a part of our team for twenty. They masterfully kept the business afloat and took care of my clients when I couldn't. I thank them both from the bottom of my heart.

I am indebted to all the medical professionals who have cared for me throughout my ordeal. In particular, I wish to thank my internist and friend Dr. Irv Johnson and his wife and nurse Cheryl for thirty years of great care, both when I felt on top of the world and when I was at the bottom of the deepest valley; Dr. Jay Morgan for putting my shattered spine back together in a way that allowed me to reclaim my life; Dr. John Davis who tirelessly cared for me for the nearly forty days I stayed in the hospital; Dr. Elaine Date for giving me hope when I thought there was none; Dr. Dieter Bruno who, by skillfully helping me through my incontinence, prostate cancer, and loss of sexual function, changed my life forever; personal trainer Michaela Lien and massage therapist Ben Cabal, my dream team, for helping me go from a wheelchair to a racing bike; licensed marriage and family therapist Anne Courtney M.A. for helping Jill and I navigate what we consider our second marriage; Dr. John Lannin and his wonderful assistant

Liza for giving me two incredible knee replacements that feel as good as the joints God gave me; Dr. David Chow for giving me a second chance by overseeing my pain management and medications; Dr. Chris Allaman who lightened my load by relieving me of the burden of wearing glasses; Dr. Parminder Sethi who made a previously complicated bathroom routine uncomplicated under his care; and Ramona and Laurel who make Dr. King's office run smoothly and took care of me on my many, many visits. I hope other people who face medical challenges are as lucky as I have been when it comes to medical practitioners and their staff.

I also wish to thank my friends John Kirsch and Dr. Jon Arnow who, by introducing me to the joys of a hand bike, opened the door to recovery.

In addition, I am thankful for Colin Smith and Erin Kelly Smith's encouragement to write this book and then helping me make it happen.

Last but not least, I thank my co-author Lori Hetherington. My only employee for the first five years of my New York Life insurance career, she was truly a critical part of my success early on. I was a newcomer to the San Francisco Bay Area with no contacts and Lori took charge of my direct mail marketing campaign to locate potential clients. Together we devised a strategy that proved effective, efficient, and profitable. Unfortunately for me, she moved to Florence Italy to start a new life but we stayed in touch.

When the idea of writing a book kept popping up, I knew I would need a lot of help. Lori and I reunited over dinner in San Francisco in 2016 and, as she had since become a translator and writer, I half-joked "maybe you can help me write a book someday." The more I thought about the book and who might be the right person to help, the more Lori made sense. She knew me well but was not too close, and she also knew Jill. Besides, I was convinced a female touch and perspective would enhance the telling of my story.

Every time I challenged her with the idea of being my co-author, saying it wouldn't be easy to deal with me, she never flinched. It was always, "I'm ready when you are." I have no doubt this book would have never gotten off the ground without Lori's involvement. She took my mediocre version and transformed it into something I'm proud of and believe can help other people. I cherish our friendship and can't thank her enough for her hand in this project.

It is with love and humility that I thank all these amazing individuals, as well as so many others who are forever in my heart, for giving me reasons to keep fighting and to stay alive.

About the authors:

William C. Wallace lives in Lafayette California with his wife, Jill. Together they have three grown sons. A founding member of the Wallace Advisory Group, his career in the financial services sector has spanned more than four decades. To read more about his personal journey go to www.abraveheartbook.com.

Lori Hetherington is a translator and writer based in Florence Italy. Her recent books include *Then She Was Born*, *The Power of Pasta*, and *Ancient Wisdom: The Monk with No Past*. For more information go to www.lhetheringtontranslation.com.

Help us spread the word by writing a review on Amazon. Simply click on "ratings" to the right of the stars and let the world know what you thought of A BRAVE HEART.

Made in the USA
San Bernardino, CA
11 August 2020